SEEKER
AFTER

Books by Idries Shah

University Lectures:

A Perfumed Scorpion (Institute for the Study of Human Knowledge
and California University)
Special Problems in the Study of Sufi Ideas (Sussex University)
The Elephant in the Dark: Christianity, Islam and the Sufis (Geneva University)
Neglected Aspects of Sufi Study: Beginning to Begin
(The New School for Social Research)

Sufi Studies and Middle Eastern Literature:

The Sufis
Caravan of Dreams
The Way of the Sufi
Tales of the Dervishes: Teaching-Stories over a Thousand Years

Traditional Psychology, Teaching Encounters and Narratives:

Thinkers of the East: Studies in Experientialism
Wisdom of the Idiots
The Dermis Probe
Learning how to Learn: Psychology and Spirituality in the Sufi Way
The Magic Monastery: Analogical and Action Philosophy

Current and Traditional Ideas:

Reflections
The Book of the Book
A Veiled Gazelle: Seeing how to See
Special Illumination: The Sufi Use of Humour

The Mulla Nasrudin Corpus:

The Exploits of the Incomparable Mulla Nasrudin
The Pleasantries of the Incredible Mulla Nasrudin
The Subtleties of the Inimitable Mulla Nasrudin

Travel and Exploration:

Destination Mecca

Studies in Minority Beliefs:

The Secret Lore of Magic
Oriental Magic (Introduction by Professor Louis Marin)

Selected Folktales and their Background:

World Tales

Translated by Idries Shah:

The Hundred Tales of Wisdom (Aflaki's *Munaqib*)

Studies of the English:

Darkest England
The Natives are Restless

SEEKER AFTER TRUTH

A *Handbook* by
IDRIES SHAH

From Tales, Discussions and Teachings, Letters and Lectures

THE OCTAGON PRESS
LONDON

**Published by the Octagon Press with the aid of
a subvention from the Sufi Trust**

ISBN 0 863040 12 8

First Published 1982
First printed in this edition 1992

*Printed and bound in Great Britain by
Redwood Press Limited, Melksham, Wiltshire*

CONTENTS

1
TALES OF THE CLASSICAL MASTERS

Praying for Rain

It is recounted among the wise that there was once a great drought at Qasr al-Arifin, and the people went to the Master Bahaudin Naqshband, asking him to pray, to ask God for rain.

He led them through the streets until he came to a place where a woman sat, nursing a small baby in her arms.

'I beg of you to feed that infant' said the Master.

'I know when to feed the child,' said the woman, 'as I am his mother. Why do you concern yourself with things which are disposed of in a manner whereof you know nothing?'

Bahaudin had the woman's words written down and read out to the crowd.

The One without the Other

It is recorded that a man went to Ahmad Yasavi, the Sufi master of Turkestan, and said:

'Teach me without books, and let me learn to understand without the intervention of a master between me and Truth, for humans are frail, and reading books does not enlighten me.'

Yasavi said:

'Do you seek to eat without a mouth, or to digest without a stomach? Perhaps you would like to walk without feet and buy without paying.... I could do as you ask only if you could first dispense with physical organs, as you wish to avoid those things which have been devised for the spiritual organs.

'Just think for a moment whether you could use food without an apparatus, approach the Sufis without having heard of them in the words you so dislike, desire wisdom without a source appropriate to your state.

'It may be an amusing pastime to think of learning without books as a basis, and experiencing without a teacher. So is it an

3

amusing pastime to think of magic and miracles. Aside from the amusement, what of the permanent yield of the activity?'

The Disobedience of Moses

According to Abu-Talib Makki, Moses related tales of how he learnt to widen his understanding, from narrow assumptions to correct perspective.

Moses was ill, and he was offered various remedies to treat the sickness. But he refused, saying that God would help him instead.

But God, it is related, commanded Moses to use medicines, saying:

'By refusing to accept the mission of the medicine, you have called into question the wisdom of him who endowed the remedies with their virtue!'

It is for this reason that there is a saying, 'Trust in God and tie your camel.' If you were expected to do nothing, why is there such a thing as a camel-hobble?

Hadrat Bahaudin Naqshband of Bokhara has said, in this connexion:

'If a withering leaf says by its appearance that it needs water and because you have the power to provide it you also have the duty to do so, these "words" of the leaf are the manifestation of the command of the creator of the leaf, and are addressed to you. If you insist upon a personal command from the Originator, ask why the means of communication has been placed before you. Is it there for you to neglect?'

Sting into Remedy

There were once two grandees in the city of Bistam who disliked one another because of some ancient rivalry. Both of them, as it happened, also wanted to study the secrets of man's origins and destiny under the renowned man of wisdom, Ali Beg, whose home

4

was in a distant part of Persia.

But Ali, before seeing them, wrote to another sage, Ibn Hamza, who lived near Bistam, and asked him to speak to them on his behalf.

But each refused to see Ibn Hamza.

The first grandee said:

'I want the root, not the branch!'

The second said:

'Ibn Hamza is a nobody'

Now Ibn Hamza began to spread scurrilous rumours about the two would-be illuminates. After some months, hearing venomous tales about themselves from all sides and having traced them to Ibn Hamza, the two aristocrats felt mutually assailed, became reconciled to one another, united in their anger against Ibn Hamza, and went to see him, full of fury. They stormed and raged at Ibn Hamza, completely forgetting every single counsel of wisdom which they had heard throughout their lives up to that time.

'Do you know why we have come to see you, despicable wretch?' they screamed, as soon as they entered Ibn Hamza's presence.

'Yes, indeed I do', answered Ibn Hamza, 'you have come:

'Firstly, because Ali Beg wanted to demonstrate how fundamentally shallow your "deep" feelings of mutual enmity are;

'Secondly, because you were required to show that your superficial feelings could easily be manipulated to make you come here even though you had individually made up your minds at first not to do so;

'Thirdly, because although disobedient to Ali Beg's orders, you could be shown that certain desires *must* be carried out;

'Fourthly, you are here so that the other people present at this moment can learn, and you can be their unwitting teacher in this transaction;

'Fifthly, because both Ali Beg and I had need of showing the poisonous local populace, riddled with suspicion and delighted at spreading rumours such as the ones which I initiated about you two, that we men of the heart are not their inevitable victims; but that we may also know how to employ their harmful actions against their harmfulness itself;

'Sixthly, you are here because, as a consequence of the foregoing events, facts and explanations, there is a prospect of transforming a sting into a remedy, and a weapon into an instrument of value.'

Weapons

Hakim al-Mansuri was a great sage of Balkh, in Central Asia. He had thousands of disciples, and his mere presence at the courts of kings was regarded as conferring legitimacy upon their rule.

But he very seldom spoke. When he did, it was about matters which did not seem to be connected with spiritual concerns. And yet many great masters of the Sufi Way attribute their attainments to having sat at his table, or from being in his guest-house, or even from associating with the other disciples, or working in his house.

One day, the Hakim was challenged by a famous preacher to dispute with him on matters of philosophy. The preacher claimed that Al-Mansuri knew nothing about wisdom, and spoke very little on weighty matters because he was ignorant of them.

Al-Mansuri set out for Herat, where the challenger, Qari Mukhtar, taught at a famous college. Each of the disputants was attended by hundreds of students, who had assembled, together with a multitude of townsfolk, to witness the duel of these giants.

The Qari – as the challenger – began his tirade with a carefully thought-out sentence, obviously preparing to launch a full-scale attack. Then, suddenly, after less than a minute, the Hakim stood up and pointed his finger at the Qari, who stood like stone, abruptly ceasing to speak. Then he fled from the hall.

On the way home, one of the disciples said to his master, who had been cheered to the echo by the delighted audience: 'Why did you choose to throw paralysis upon that man, instead of refuting his arguments?'

The Hakim answered: 'If you have a sword in your hand, do you charge the opponent with mud bricks? Even a monkey would not chatter if it could do something more effective. That man wanted to defeat me, not to discover truth.'

Elephant-meat

Ibrahim Khawas* relates this instruction-narrative, which has been used to test the understanding of students of Sufism:

'In company with a number of Sufis, I was making a journey on shipboard when we were wrecked, and I found myself, with some others, just able to reach a desolate shore.

'We did not know where we were, neither did we have any food. It seemed that we would be likely to perish, as days passed without any sign of succour.

'We discussed the position and decided that each of us would make a vow to do some good, or to abandon some evil which cut him off from his Lord. In this way, we thought, the exercise of sincerity might be the means of providing escape from helplessness.

'Each one made his oath: one that from now on he would carry out fasting, another one that he would pray so many times each day, and yet another one that he would carry out pilgrimages on foot. Everyone in this way made his declaration and compact that he would abstain from some indulgence, or else that he would do something of religious worth.

'Now it came to me to declare my vow, and I was asked by the others to speak. I wanted to make my promise, and it came into my mind, without any thought or consideration, that I would say: "I shall not eat any elephant-meat".

'The others exclaimed: "This is no time for joking and amusement; no time for such things, as we remain in this danger of death".

'I answered: "By God, I did not say this in the spirit you mention. While you were talking I thought over all the possible good actions I might do, and all the bad things I might avoid – and something prevented me from choosing one of them. And what I have just said simply came to me without any reflection, and I said

---

* IBRAHIM KHAWAS (Abu-Ishaq Ibrahim ibn Ahmad al-Khawas, *The Palm-Weaver*) died in 910 of the Christian Era. He was an associate of Junaid of Baghdad and of Nuri.

Khawas's name is associated with teaching narratives which are understood at the ordinary level and also lead to deeper understanding of man. The present story is preserved in Al-Tanukhi's book *Al-Faraj ba'd al-shidda* written in the 10th century, whose name may be translated as *Release after Hardship*. The story exemplifies just this; and although placed in a travel tale frame, it is allegorical of the right and wrong ways to approach, and also to assess, human development and intention.

7

it. It is possible that some divine Wisdom has put the idea into my head and has allowed me to speak in this way."

'The party then decided to explore further into the land where they were cast, to look for food. After arranging for a central point at which to reassemble, and that anything found should be shared, they started their search.

'They had not gone far when my friends found a young elephant, and decided that they could survive if they killed it to eat. The animal was slaughtered, and the meat was cooked over a fire. Although they asked me to share the food, I was unable to do so, and I answered: "You are all witnesses that I have made the vow to abstain from this very thing, and I cannot break that oath. It may even be that God has caused me to think of this particular vow so that I might die. In any case, it is unlawful to break my oath."

'After eating, everyone lay down to sleep; and soon we heard the trumpeting of an infuriated elephant bearing down upon us. The noise was so great that the earth shook, and all were terrified. Since it seemed obvious that everyone was to be killed, they gave up hope, and murmured their Confesssion of Faith, as people do when faced by death.

'Now the elephant, when he reached us, extended his trunk to each traveller in turn, smelling him. One by one, as he smelt the odour of roast elephant-meat, he stamped the man to death, until he came to me.

'I lay on the ground, repeating my *Shahada* (Confession), in mortal terror. The elephant smelt me again and again, not as hastily as he had done with the others. Then he caught me up in his trunk, and I imagined that he was going to kill me in some way different from the others. But he placed me on his back, where I sat, and started to move away, sometimes walking, sometimes running, covering a long distance.

'I was extremely uncomfortable on the animal's back, yet I began to think that perhaps I might be able in some way to escape.

'It was dawn when the elephant took me down and placed me on the earth, running off in the direction from which we had come. I could not understand the reason for his actions, and was still in fear. But eventually he vanished over the horizon.

'Giving thanks for my deliverance, I offered prayers and thanks to the Lord; and when I felt the heat of the day I looked up and realised that I was beside a broad highway.

'I went along the road and after some time came to a populous city, where I related all that had happened to the people, who were most surprised and said that it was a distance of ordinarily several days from which the elephant had brought me.

8

'After spending some time in that city and recovering from my exhaustion, I was able to return to my own land in safety and health.'

Generosity

The great teacher Sahl of Tustar, relates that God told Moses that real self-sacrifice for the sake of others is the basis of the greatest capacity for perception of the divine: the extreme self-sacrifice which was given to Mohammed and his followers.

Imam Ghazzali relates, in the Third Book of his *Revival of Religious Sciences,* how a man who was famed as generous learnt what generosity really was:

THE BLACK SLAVE AND THE DOG

Abdullah Ibn Ja'far owned an orchard and went one day to visit it. He passed through a vineyard, where he saw a black slave sitting, with some bread in front of him and a dog nearby.

As Abdullah watched, the slave took a piece of the bread and threw it to the dog, which ate it. Then he gave it another piece, and another.

Abdullah asked:

'How much bread are you given every day?'

The slave answered:

'That quantity which you have just seen eaten by the dog.'

'Why', Abdullah asked, 'do you give it to a dog, instead of attending first to your own need?'

'There are no dogs hereabouts' said the black man, 'and this one has come from a great distance and is hungry. Because of this I did not desire to eat my bread.'

'But how will you manage for food today?' asked the generous Abdullah.

'I shall endure the hunger!' said the black.

Abdullah thought, 'I am the one who has the reputation for generosity, and yet this slave is more philanthropic.'

He bought the vineyard and gave it to the slave, also buying his freedom and releasing him.

Grouping

There was once a King, who visited the Sage Bahaudin Naqsh-band, 'The Designer', and sat observing his assembly.

Afterwards, when they were eating, the King said:

'Teacher of the Age! Your disciples, when you are in Session, are ranged in semicircles, and in an orderly manner very similar to that of my own Court. Is there any significance in this?'

Bahaudin answered:

'King of the World! How are your own courtiers stationed? Tell me, and I shall describe the ordering of the ranks of the Seekers.'

'The first arc' said the King, 'is composed of those who are in especial favour with me, so that they are nearest. The second array comprises the most important and powerful people in the realm, and the ambassadors. The outer rank is for all the lesser ones.'

'In that case,' said the Shah, 'Our marshalling of the people is far from the intention expressed by you. Those nearest to me are the deaf, so they they shall hear. The middle group is composed of the ignorant, so that they may pay attention to the Teaching. Farthest away are the Enlightened, for whom proximity of this kind is unimportant.'

Scent and Reality

The Master Bahaudin was sitting one evening after dinner, sur-rounded by a large number of newcomers, old and young, all eager to learn.

A silence fell, and the Master asked for a question.

Someone said:

'What is the greatest difficulty in the learning and the teaching of the Way?'

The Master answered:

'People go by superficialities. They are attracted by preaching, by rumour and report, and by that which excites them – like bees to the scent of flowers.'

The man asked:

'But how else are people to approach wisdom, or bees, flowers?'

The Master answered:

'The human approaches wisdom through report and noise, preaching and reading and excitement. After he has approached it, however, he stays near it to demand more of the same: not whatever it can give, which is what it is there for.

'Bees approach flowers by scent, but they do not, once arrived at the proximity of the bloom, demand merely more and more scent. They adjust to the nectar, which they have to collect. This is the equivalent of the reality of wisdom, of which the report and imaginings are as it were the scent.

'So the number of "real bees" among humanity is very small. Whereas almost all bees are bees, in being able to collect nectar, almost all human beings are not yet human beings in the sense of being attuned to perceive what they were created for.'

Then the Master said:

'Let those who came here, to Qasr al-Arifin, because of reading stand up.'

Many stood.

'Let those,' he continued, 'who came to us because of hearing about us also stand up'.

Many more stood.

'Those who are still seated,' he continued, 'are those who came because they perceived our presence and authenticity in another, subtle, manner.

'Those who are standing, old and young, include many who only demand more and more of their feelings to be stirred, who desire excitement or calm. Before they can learn what they cannot experience elsewhere, they must require knowledge and not services of attraction.'

He then said:

'There are those who are attracted to a teacher because of his repute, and who accordingly travel to see him, to seek even more of the same sensation. When he dies, they visit his grave, again for a similar reason.

'Unless their aspirations are transformed, as if by alchemy, they will not find truth.

'And,' he said, 'there are those who visit a teacher not because they have heard of him as a great living mentor; not because they wish to see his tomb, but because they recognise his inmost Reality. One day everyone will possess this faculty.'

Now Bahaudin the Designer said:

'But in the meantime the work which will be done eventually through the generations has to be performed in one and the same individual. To become a Moses you will have to transcend your Pharaoh. The man who is attracted by repute must become, as it

11

were, another man. He must become a man who stays in proximity to wisdom because he has sensed its inmost Reality.

'This is the purpose of this Work before he can learn. Until he has learnt this, he is a mere dervish. A dervish desires, a Sufi perceives.'

The Heretics

It is related that Imam al-Ghazali was invited one day to an assembly of jurists, whose chief said to him:

'You are a learned man, as we are also from among the learned. Therefore humbler folk come to you to seek interpretations of the *Sharia*, the Holy Law. It has been reported to us that you have advised some of these people not to observe the fast during the month of Ramadan. You are also said to have stated that certain people should not make the pilgrimage to Mecca. Others have averred that you have reprimanded people for saying "There is no God but Allah". Such mischievous words, if true, are proof to us of infidelity. Only your reputation has so far protected you from death for apostasy. The people have a right to be protected from such as you.'

Ghazali sighed and answered:

'The Holy Law of Islam itself says that people who are not of a full understanding of the Law and what it means are not culpable under that Law, nor subject to its rules. These include children and imbeciles, but must also include those bereft of understanding. If a man does not perceive the inner reality of fasting, or goes on a pilgrimage only to suffer, or says the Confession of Faith and has no faith, he is bereft of understanding, and should not be encouraged to continue, but must be put on the road to understanding. The people, in your words, have the right to be protected from such as you, who would reward them for no merit and persecute them for no crime.

'If a man cannot walk by reason of having a lame leg, do you tell him to walk, or do you give him a crutch or heal his affliction?

'It is due to his foretelling of the appearance of such as you that the Prophet has said: "Islam came as a stranger and it will depart as a stranger." Understanding of the meaning of things is beyond your intention, your training and your capacity. That is why there

12

is nothing left to you but to threaten people with death for apostasy. And yet it is not I who am the apostate, but you.'

Neighbour

Imam Abu-Hanifa was one of the great Sufis, and is recognised as the founder of the Hanifite School of Law. He was so independent that he would never go to Court, although the Caliph tried everything to attract the interest of the most illustrious sage of the time.

Abu-Hanifa had a neighbour, a cobbler who was also a considerable drunkard. Every night the wild ravings of the alcoholic disturbed his meditations, but the Imam did not complain.

One night there was no sound from the cobbler's room, and the Imam, going to enquire about his welfare, found that the imperial police had arrested him. He immediately went to the palace to see the Caliph Mansour.

At the sight of the Imam the guards sprang to attention, the officers and courtiers bowed, and the Emirs rose from their places. The Caliph went to the door of the throne-room to receive Abu-Hanifa, and brought him to the throne itself, and seated him upon it.

'May I know the reason for the honour of this visit?' the Caliph asked.

'The cobbler from next door has been arrested, and I come to ask for his release' said the Imam.

'But' said the Captain of the Guard, 'this man is a disorderly drunkard.'

'This man,' said the Imam, 'is without friends, and is my neighbour.'

'Illustrious Imam' said the Caliph; 'your nobility of spirit must receive its true recognition. You intercede for one prisoner. Our generosity matches yours: I hereby release every single prisoner in the empire of Islam.'

Teaching

The Sufi sage Saadi of Shiraz was on his way to Baghdad, when the caravan which he was with was attacked by bandits.

When the robbers asked him for his possessions, Saadi handed their chief a pile of books and some gold coins. 'I give these to you as a gift, so do not regard them as stolen' he said, 'but make good use of them.'

The robbers sneered, and their chief said: 'I suppose you are trying to teach us goodness?'

'No' said Saadi, 'I do not think that I can teach you anything. So I am hoping that I can give you these items, books and money, freely and that in return you will do something for me with them.'

'And what is that?'

'Find a wise man, give him these books and pay his upkeep. Let him at least teach your children about the evils of theft, so that they may not repeat your mistakes.'

The Four Types

It is related that Bahaudin Naqshband was asked about the various kinds of people pursuing higher knowledge.

He said: 'I shall tell you by means of an allegory, not to be taken as literally true, but reflecting the condition of the human being.'

Then he told this story:

It is recorded in the traditions of the Lovers of Truth, that when the souls were created, before the bodies, they were asked what they wanted as a means of travelling in this world.

There were four parties among them. The first desired to travel on foot, as the safest method. The second desired horses, for this would mean less work for them. The third wished to travel on the wind, to overcome limitations. The fourth chose light, by which they could understand as well as move.

These four groups still exist, and all people still abide by one of these characteristics. Those who are the pedestrians are limited in space and speed. They are the imitators. The horsemen are those who rely on books, and are thus driven by the horse of the author's beliefs. The third category are blown all over the place as if by the

14

wind, and the fourth are the Sufis.

In terms of studies, the first group attach themselves to lower and exciting cults; the second to zealously propagated ideas; the third to systems of their own choosing or devising, taking something here and something else there; the fourth are the Sufis.

We can judge the ability of the people by the choice which they have made of travelling. The first group are interested in what they think are techniques; the second in exciting thoughts and reports; the third in one thing after another – and the fourth recognise the true Sufic reality.

The Fires of Today...

It is related that Bahaudin Naqshband said:

'I was invited to speak at an assembly of the educated and the ignorant. There arrived a very large collection of people, attentive and interested, but as I looked and felt, I did not at that time see a single "human being".

'I said to the people whom I had taken with me, in order to demonstrate the limitations of action upon the unsuitable:

"A well is not filled by means of dew, and a leaf will not be found after being deluged with the contents of a well."

'I started by saying:

"Sufis are a disgrace. They have secret teachings which they keep from the ordinary people. The eminence which many Sufis attain is due to the exercise of forbidden powers. Now tell me, do you want to be a Sufi?"

'Almost all of those present shook their heads.

'Then I continued:

"Such were the words spoken by the ignorant, foolish and block-headed Governor of Kufa, of whom you all know much. As you are aware, he was a bigot, a murderer and an enemy of humanity. It is small wonder that he felt the need to represent the Sufis in this manner.

"Now all of us here know that the Sufis are the elect of humankind. Who among you dares to call himself a Sufi?"

'At these words, everyone rose.

'Thus does pomposity (*ab o tab*) stem from vanity (*ghurur*), which is a manifestation of the Commanding Self (*nafs i ammara*).

'The fires of today are the ashes of tomorrow.'

15

The Law of
Reverse Effect

A man once visited Al-Shah, Bahaudin Naqshband, saying that he wanted directions on how to behave, on how to live his life, on what to do and what not to do.

The Master called some of his disciples to dinner and asked the man to put his questions again.

When this had been done, Sheikh Bahaudin said:

'You should try to live an easy life, supporting yourself by stealing, and bringing part of the money to me. You should neglect prayer and tidiness of appearance and should always try to get the upper hand over other people. In short, lack of principles and cunning should see you through.'

As the Master spoke, the applicant was becoming more and more uneasy; as soon as he had finished, he ran from the room.

Some weeks later, Bahaudin asked whether there was any news of his would-be disciple. 'Yes', they told him, 'he is living an exemplary life, in Samarkand. He also tells everyone that you are Satan, and tried to wean him from the Right Path.'

Bahaudin laughed. 'If I had told him to live a good life,' he said, 'he would not have obeyed, because all the injunctions so to do have been dinned into him from babyhood. In reality he hankered for something more strange, and when I assailed his inward self with an account of a strange way of life, he realised that he would feel better as a compliant and virtuous man.'

'But' asked his disciple, 'what of his blackening your name, as an adviser in sin?'

'Those who believe evil, partake in evil,' said the Master. 'And I am sure that the scholars of Samarkand are not such people.'

Treasure

It is related of the most ancient Sufis, and repeated by many who followed them, throughout the schools which have formed and dissolved and formed again, that the Anecdote of the Treasure works within the mind to bring understanding of deep things to those who believe only that shallow feelings are deep, and that low things are high, and that what is on the surface is what is on the inside:

THE TREASURE

Several men went to a teaching Master and clamoured for his attention, each vying with the other to ask his question, or to make his statement, or to get his answer.

When the Master had produced order in this multitude,

The First man said:

'I have been seeking for many years, and I have found nothing.'

The Second man said:

'I have found delight in the seeking: is this then its purpose?'

The Third man said:

'Sometimes I think that I have found, and then I feel that I have not, and that I must continue.'

The Fourth man said:

'Sometimes I doubt myself, sometimes the teachers, sometimes the Truth itself.'

The Master answered:

'There may be a hundred questions, but there is only one answer, and I shall now give it and inform you all. This is it:

'There were a number of men who were attracted to the design of digging for a treasure. They took all sorts of implements and went to the place where it was buried, and they started to work. Some tired easily, which made them feel that the task might not be worth while. Some found small fragments of clay pots and from time to time thought that this must be the treasure itself. Some enjoyed for the first time the pleasures of hard work, which they imagined to be the delights of seeking or of finding. Some, again, looked at the mud and the stones, and were distressed by their abundance, for they were people easily dispirited.

'And there were many other men, and women too, who felt many things, for they had put a time or a shape upon the work, and when the time was passed, or the shape, as they thought, found, they became a prey to delusion and agitation.

'Those who persisted found the container which held the precious hoard; those who were victims of confusion and debate did not. The confused ones passed the rest of their days in seeking information and explanations, but the dedicated bore off the treasure.

'So those who were agitated and deluded stumbled from one sage to another, asking how they might know the treasure, how they might seek it, how they might find it. The sages, one and all,

17

told them that they could not do any of these things unless they were as those who had succeeded. But the people clamoured for success, not for guidance, as they were already convinced that they possessed, from the start, the mind, the body and the spirit which would enable them to bring their design to fruitful conclusion.'

Permission to Expound

Because of the special nature of Sufi writings, teachers of the Way have often issued permissions to expound and to explain their books to worthy individuals.

Not everyone, of course, has abided by this requirement, and many have been the supposed Sufis who have made a career for themselves by purporting to be able to teach through the books of Sufi masters.

It is related that a dervish was holding forth on one of the illustrious poet Jami's works one day, when a newcomer slipped into the lecture-hall and started to shake his head more and more often, as the learned one gave his interpretations of the meaning of Jami.

Everyone was looking at the stranger, and finally the dervish fixed him with a penetrating eye and cried:

'Do you presume to disagree with me?'

'Yes' said the other man.

'And,' asked the dervish, 'have you permission from the Great Master Jami to interpret his works?'

'No'.

'Then who are you, and by what right do you behave in this ridiculous manner, challenging a man of my importance?'

'My name is Jami' said the visitor, and slipped away.

2
QUESTIONS AND
ANSWERS

Not their Way, but *their* Way

Q: I have heard the phrase used by Sufis, 'Not their way, but their way.' What can this possibly mean?

A: It is a technical term, and an extremely useful one. It refers to an account of something which has a meaning in a dimension which is not understood by conventional thinkers. There are two 'they's. The first lot in the phrase, are the ordinary people. The second are those who work in another dimension.

Take such a narrative as this:

HOW CAN HUMAN ACTIONS BE DIVINE?

It is related (and quoted in, for example, Hujwiri's *Revelation of the Veiled*) that the Prophet said:

'There is many a one with dirty hair, dust-stained, clad in two old garments, whom men never heed; but if he were to swear by God, God would verify his oath.'

Such a statement appears to suggest that the person mentioned either was God, which is impossible according to most people; or commanded God, which is even more impossible; or that he was acting in direct harmony with God in such a way as to know the divine decrees or to initiate terrestrial action in an interventionist manner: both highly questionable possibilities according to most human belief.

The fact is, however, that the meaning of the exact nature of this individual's activities and their harmonization with divine intention are not to be understood in 'their' (the intellectuals') way, but in 'their' (the perceptives') way.

The Sufi poet Jami, in some especially beautiful lines, says:
Whether seeker of evil or good
Whether inmate of a monastery or cloister
From the viewpoint of Form, all is other than He!
From the viewpoint of Truth, all is none other than He!

But remember, too, that Shabistari says:

21

To whomever the Divine has not shown the Way
It will not be revealed to him through logic.

Prayers and Rituals

*Q: I have read that Gharib Nawaz, quoting Master Samnun
Muhibb, said that the really illuminated are 'The people who have
nothing to do with outward prayers, rituals or ascetic life, but are
the people given to devotion and contemplation.' Why should one
not pray? What is wrong with rituals? Who should not be an
ascetic?*

A: When prayer, rituals and ascetic life are just a means of
self-indulgence, they are harmful rather than beneficial. This is
quite obvious to people nowadays, when it is widely recognised
that fixations are not the same as valuable and laudable obser-
vances. One should not pray if that prayer is vanity; rituals are
wrong when they provide lower satisfactions, like emotional
stimulus instead of enlightenment; he or she should not be an
ascetic who is only enjoying it.

These facts have been known for a very long time, and have
been alluded to by spiritual teachers. From time to time, in
default of teaching structures which can help people to avoid the
traps which these activities lay for the unworthy, people of all religions have let the cause go by default, and have assumed that
someone is holy if carrying out some or all of these activities.

The True and the
False Sufi

*Q: I have read that the great Sufi Gazur-Ilahi quoted, with
approval, Sheikh Yahya Munir as follows:*

'There is no uniform behaviour amongst the Masters. One may
eat and sleep well, another will fast and sit up all night. One may
spend time with people, another holds himself aloof. One will be
found dressed in rags and another in silks and linen of high
quality; one is silent, another speaks animatedly. One will conceal

22

his saintship, another will show it publicly. One of them will serve all human beings, both the devout and the debauched: and another will have no truck with the evil. . . .'

Q: *If this is so, how are we to know the true Sufi, and why should Sufis behave in such disparate ways?*

A: Sufis behave in any way which is necessary to their fulfilling their function; so you would expect a wide variation in behaviour. Again, remember that the things of the world referred to by Sheikh Yahya are superficial, secondary and not essential to the Sufi, hence he has only a secondary and relatively unimportant personal connexion with them. This is why they behave differently, one from the other: or even the same individual at different times.

As to the problem of recognising a true *Sufi*, this is no problem to the true *person*. You have read the passage which you have just quoted to me, but perhaps you have not read enough in Sufi writings to record that Sufis say that you will only be misled if something unworthy in yourself attracts you to an unworthy person. It is not for the Sufi to represent himself as worthy; it is not for anyone to give you a test for a Sufi. It is for whoever wants to discern truth to focus that part of himself or herself which is honest towards the supposed Sufi. Like calls to like, truth to truth and deceit to deceit. If you are not yourself deceitful, you will not be deceived. The assumption, you know, that all seekers are honest and that they only need a test to ascertain the honesty of a spiritual teacher is very much out of line with the real facts.

A Ruse

Q: *People say that you say and do things – such as opposing scholars – which cause confusion and enmity. Why should you do this?*

A: I can only give you the story of Saadi, in his *Bostan*, that recalls one aspect of this situation. There was once an old man whom a youth had helped with a small sum of money. One day he saw the young man being led by an escort of soldiers to his execution, for something which he was supposed to have done.

The ancient immediately cried out: 'The King is dead!' This caused such confusion and panic among the troops that the youth was able to escape.

Eventually, however, the old man was arrested and brought

before the king, who asked him: 'Why should you do such a thing, and why should you wish me dead?'

The ancient replied: 'My calling out that you were dead did not hurt you at all, but it saved a life.'

The king was so amazed by this tale that he set the old man free, I am glad to say.

Instrumental

Q: What are the roles of rituals and beliefs and studies for the Sufi?

A: To be a Sufi and to study the Way is to have a certain attitude. This attitude is produced by the effect of Sufi teachers, who exercise the instrumental function in relation to the Seeker. Rituals and beliefs, and studies, can only have an instrumental effect suitable for Sufi progress when they are correctly used, and by people who are not affected by them in the customary manner.

This has all been very clearly laid down by Abul' Hasan Nuri, over a thousand years ago:

'A Sufi' he says, 'is one who is not bound by anything nor does he bind anything'. This means that he does what he does from free choice and not from compulsion or conditioning. Equally, he is not attached to things and does not bind others to him. Nuri continues: 'Sufism is not a doctrine or worldly knowledge. If it were ceremonial, this would have to be practised (regularly). If it were ordinary learning, it would have to be taught by formal methods. In fact, it is a matter of disposition.'

This disposition is the 'attitude' which I have mentioned, which is attained by the instrumental function, not by attachment or rituals.*

Vicissitudes of a Teaching

Q: If there is a single, original Teaching, how is it that it becomes confused and misused as it passes through generations and cultures?

*Quoted by Fariduddin Attar in his *Memorials of the Saints*.

24

A: There is a saying, 'Whatever goes into a salt-mine becomes salt.' The Teaching is the worldly manifestation of something, and as such a manifestation it is affected by the deforming character in appearance and operation of those who adopt it into their culture without understanding its inner dimensions. Listen to what happened to Marhuma:

Fariduddin Attar relates in his *Ilahi-Nama* (Book of the Divine) that there was once a woman of virtue named Marhuma, which means 'She upon whom mercy is exercised.' Her fate stands for the vicissitudes of the Teaching.

Her husband decided to perform the Pilgrimage to Mecca, and left her in the care of his younger brother. After a time, this man fell in love with her, and made approaches to her. She rebuked him: but he threatened that if she did not submit he would put her in danger. When she still refused to yield, he bought four false witnesses, charging her with adultery. The woman, brought before the judge, was declared guilty and was taken to an open space to be stoned to death.

Marhuma was left for dead, and lay in that place all night. In the morning, when she began to revive, and when she was almost back to her senses, a desert Arab who was passing heard her groans. He asked her who she was, and she answered that she was ill, so he decided to take care of her.

After a few days she recovered and, seeing her beauty, the Arab besought her to marry him. 'But I am already married' she said. She so moved him by her entreaties to leave her alone that he adopted her, making her his sister.

Now the Arab had a slave, and this man fell in love with Marhuma; but she resisted him as well. He decided to have his revenge for being rebuffed. The master had a beautiful child and the slave, one night, killed it and put the bloodstained dagger which he had used under Marhuma's pillow.

When the child's mother went in the morning to give it milk, she discovered the murder: and she found the weapon in Marhuma's bed.

The Arab asked Marhuma why she had repaid his kindness in this way: giving evil in exchange for good; but she was able to convince him that she was innocent.

But the Arab realised that, after the shock which she had had, his wife would always associate Marhuma's face with the death of her little one, and so he had to send Marhuma away.

The manifestation of the Teaching, in the form of tales and exercises, of actions and thoughts, will always be as vulnerable as Marhuma, and is as often betrayed and misunderstood by the base and the ignorant. Supposed forms of Sufi teaching are abundant;

some of them have a fair face, others are associated with unacceptable histories; and these are all the result of the kind of thing which happened to Marhuma when her husband was away.

Present and Absent

Q: I find it rather difficult to get answers to my questions, both from you and from other people whom I respect. I have spent days 'sitting at the feet' of some people of great renown, and never heard them utter a word. Can you shed any light on this?

A: This question has often been asked – and answered – before. Not only has Rumi said: 'No answer is itself an answer', but the smallest lesson which we can learn from visiting a sage and getting no answer is: 'A Sufi is not a slot-machine, to be activated at your will and pleasure.'

As for the answers themselves: you will not only have to reconcile yourself, as have millions of better people, to answers *when* you can get them; you will have to use to the best advantage whatever answer the teacher happens to give you – and it may appear completely irrelevant, banal, unacceptable or insensitive. It is never any of these things.

Ancient Traditions

Q: I know that the Sufi Path is followed by Moslems, and also that many classical teachers among them have had Christian, Jewish and other disciples: there is plenty of evidence of this, which sets Sufism apart from purely theology-bound mysticism and gives it a special place in the world. But, although the Sufis say that Sufism has always existed, is there any evidence that the Prophet Mohammed himself alluded to any of the practices, such as Taubat (turning back, repentance) or Khidmat (Service) or Sabr (Patience) – the 'Stations' which the masters and the orders require people to take up for the purpose of following the Path?

A: Of course there is. You have to remember that Islam is not presented as a new religion, but as a continuation of the perennial faith. There is therefore (and must be) a continuum between ancient teaching and the standard Islamic period and afterwards. As an illustration I shall give you the story, from the Islamic Authentic Traditions, which actually embodies all three 'Stations', of *Taubat, Khidmat* and *Sabr*. It is entitled:

RECITAL OF THE CAVE (Hadith al-Ghar)

In his Discourse on Miracles, Hujwiri* related from the Traditions that one day some of the Prophet's companions asked him to relate a tale of the peoples of ancient times.

He recited:

Three people were on a journey, and when night fell they went into a cave to sleep. While they were there, there was an avalanche, and a rock blocked the entrance to the cave, trapping them.

They decided that only a miracle could save them, and that they should invoke God, asking that their altruism should be witness to their eligibility for release from what would otherwise become a tomb.

One of them accordingly said:

'I had only a goat in this world, and I used to milk it to provide something for my parents, and I also collected firewood to sell to buy food for my father and mother and myself.

'One evening when I arrived home, I found that the old couple had fallen asleep. I prepared their food and milk and stood by them, without eating anything, until they woke next morning. After that, I also ate and sat down.

'O Lord, if I have spoken the truth, help us and send release in our predicament!'

And then, as they watched, the rock moved a little, and a crack could be seen, letting in the light.

But they could not get through the small crevice, and the second man began his tale:

'I was once greatly in love with a very beautiful girl, who was blind. She refused to marry me, and so I collected money and sent her a large amount of gold with a message that she could have it if she would spend one night with me. She came, but the fear of God came into me: I turned away and allowed her to keep the money.

'O Lord, if I have spoken the truth, help us and send release in our predicament!'

As the travellers watched, the rock at the cave's aperture moved again, and the crevice became wider, though there was still not enough room for the trapped men to go forth.

*Ali al-Hujwiri, *Revelation of the Veiled*, Discourse on Miracles.

Then the third man spoke:

'At one time I hired several men to complete a certain task. When this was finished, all of them came for their money, except for one, who went away, and I did not know why or where.

'I put his wages aside, and with the money bought a sheep. As the years passed the sheep multiplied, until there was a considerable flock of them.

'Some years later the labourer appeared again, and said that he wanted his money.

'I said: "Go and take all those sheep – they are yours."

'He thought at first that I was making fun of him, but I explained what had happened, and he took the sheep away.

'O Lord, if I have spoken the truth, help us and send release in our predicament!'

As soon as he had spoken, the rock rolled from the cave's mouth and the three men were able to leave it.

Now you will see that the story concerns the man who exercised the Sufi principle of *Sabr*, patience; the man who turned away, who was practising *Taubat*, repentance; and the man who performed service, *Khidmat*, for his fellow man and in the cause of honesty.

The story illustrates the relative efficacies of three distinct Sufi practices, that they are linked (via the 'three men') and that they have effect in a certain order.

And it dates from a time before the promulgation of Islam as an historical institution as we know it. Islam itself refers back constantly to the heritage of mankind in spirituality and so, of course, do Sufis.

The Mother of Opposition

Q: When Jalaluddin Rumi says that 'Things which are seemingly opposed may in fact be working together', he is referring to the essential identity of opposites. Surely this is a formula for our solving the problems of enmity? Surely, by opposing nothing, we may get closer to that which is Real?

A: Rumi's words may indeed be sloganized into some such phrase as 'Ignorance is the Mother of Opposition'.

But to oppose nothing and to seek from such an action (or lack of it) some personal benefit carries an untrue assumption. This assumption is that the individual, this non-opposer, is capable of learning from what happens next. Why do you assume that? Certainly experience is against it, in our field at any rate.

Magical thinking assumes that because something happens in conjunction with something else, the two are connected. Thus, when a magically-minded person sees a flight of birds followed by a flash of lightning, he or she may imagine that birds cause electricity. This we know to be absurd, because everyone can test it. Similarly, the assumption that because non-opposition is found in certain situations, it can be applied as an instrument of some kind, is magical thinking, no less.

'Things nominally opposed may be working together.' Yes – and they also may not. Further, that co-operation of seemingly opposed things may or may not involve you. The fact is that, if you were sensitive enough to this concept to profit from it, you would not so readily assume that you can use it. You would already know about the qualification that other elements come into the picture. To understand which things are nominally opposed and working together, and what – if any – functions you yourself may have in such a relationship, you have to learn other things first. Rumi may have stated the fact: others have to earn the understanding of this fact in operation. And that is one of the things for which Sufi activity is organized.

Science and Omniscience

Q. *Ghazzali speaks of the 'Revitalising of the Sciences of Religion', and other great Sufis constantly refer to Sufism as a science. But since science deals in known and verifiable facts, in repeatable experiments and in the preference of reality over opinion, how can the Sufis be called 'scientific'?*

A: I do not know where you found your descriptions of science. Scientists today, and particularly historians of science, are at pains to assert that each one of the criteria which you adduce are, or have been, absent from science. Many things accepted as facts by science are hypotheses which fit all or most cases encountered. When new cases which do not fit appear, the 'facts' are changed, and new theories emerge, to be superseded in their turn. As for

29

repeatable experiments, the Sufis never do anything else than repeat what has already been determined. And there are numerous instances of supposedly scientific attitudes being seen in the end to be matters of opinion.

The outstanding scientist William Thomson (who later became Lord Kelvin) declared that Darwin's theory of evolution was impossible scientifically, since if the world were as old as all that, the Sun would have burnt out. This was, of course, an opinion. It is experience which teaches, not controversy based on supposed logic and assumptions of what is likely to be true. Both the scientists and the Sufis are, at best, people of experience. When they have experience of the reality of what they are doing, they accept it. The main difference is only that scientists are still learning, still developing their knowledge, and the Sufis have already learnt. The scientists have to update their knowledge with new discoveries, and actually do so. The body of knowledge and practice of the Sufis is not updated because its assertions and activities are not effectively challenged: they have been completed. So here you have the difference between three areas: the cult, the science and the Sufis. In a cult, new information is not admitted, because it may disturb the cult; in science, new information must be included, because science is incomplete; in Sufism, no new material is needed, since the body of knowledge is already complete. The misunderstandings arise because people put all these things into the wrong categories. They imagine that science is like Sufism, in being complete; that Sufism is like a cult, which would cause it to exclude 'new' knowledge instead of verifying it; that a cult is like science, in being open to new ideas, whereas a cult only adapts, and does not adopt, new materials.

Sufism is education, in that it has a body of knowledge which it transmits to those who have not got it. Science is like a cult when it thinks that it is omniscient. Deteriorated science is a cult, so is imitative or deteriorated Sufism. So, according to how it is handled, Sufi ideas can be demoted into a cult, and so can science and education. The main thing to remember here is that, when a cult has formed, we are no longer dealing with Sufism or science, but with a cult. Equally, when people who have been scientists or cultists approach the insights of Sufism, they cease to have the limitations which scientists and cultists have, and have therefore to be regarded, at least incipiently, as Sufis.

Keeping People Away

Q: How can teaching be carried on by Sufis if they behave as did the classical master Sari al-Saqati, who is reported to have prayed when surrounded by seekers: 'O Lord! Give them knowledge which will keep them away from me.'

A: The great Junaid of Baghdad, too, said: 'When you see the Sufi addressing the populace, know that he is empty' – as reported by the authoritative compiler Kalabadhi.

These apparently mysterious utterances are, in reality, simplicity itself to understand.

In the case of Saqati, he is speaking of the 'me' which is attracting the people: the external him, which he knows to be what they are curious about, and which is the superficiality. If the people get the knowledge to keep away from that 'me' – to stop crowding around like yokels at a circus – then they can begin to learn from the inwardness of Saqati.

Similarly with Junaid, he is speaking of someone who will harangue the multitude and therefore can only speak of generalities and of things which will please the public. The real Sufi will, like any expert or skilled person, be best able to teach those who have a grounding of the subject.

People who have made some study of Sufism, or who think that they have, are always trying to teach. This is a stage in the life of the learner, not of the teacher. This is why Sufis have said, 'I longed to teach, but I had to wait until the desire had left me before I could really do so.'

Even people of great repute suffer from such vanity as obscures from themselves the fact that trying to teach can be a snare set by vanity.

THE BEGGAR AND THE COAT

The great Abu-Hafs was asked by his disciple for permission to teach. The master agreed, and sat in the audience at his first lecture.

When the disciple, Abu-Uthman, had finished, a beggar came forward. Abu-Uthman, before he could say anything, gave him his coat.

The master stood up and called out:

'You liar! Do not speak to men while you have this thing in you!'

Abu-Uthman asked:

'What thing?'

The master told him:

'You are gratifying yourself, and you are forestalling the needy man's need to ask humbly, for his own sake.'

The beggar and the disciple have much in common: they must each come to the stage where they are prepared to ask. And it is this posture which gives them the focus of mind within which to be able to receive correctly.

Parable of the King and the Youth

Q: If the Sufis are uncaring about things of this world, why is it that so many of them have been so illustrious in art, science, state-craft and literature?

A: The Sufis are uncaring about things of this world when such things are attached to vanity and regarded as vitally important beyond their real significance. But the Sufis work *in* the world, and therefore *with* 'things of the world'.

There are many ways of working in and with the world unexpected by ordinary people, who do not see all the cause-and-effect relationships of people, events and things.

The most familiar story concerning this is the one in which Khidr taught Moses by taking him on a journey and performing various inexplicable actions.

And the Sufi, too, has to be protected in the world, to an extent, by his own awareness: 'like the camel in the desert' as the phrase has it, indicating adjustment to the environment.

There is a tale connected with this in the ancient classic, the *Laila and Majnun* of Nizami:

There was once a king, who took as a boon companion a certain youth, and was most attached to him.

Now this youth, in spite of all the protestations of the king, realised that he was not trustworthy. He used to go every day and feed the royal dogs, a pack of savage brutes.

One day the king became enraged at the young man, and ordered him to be thrown to the dogs. But they, because they knew him so well, refused to do him any harm.

Biographers and Saints

Q: Many Sufis, including Jami, Saadi and Hujwiri, wrote as mere biographers of the great teachers. Yet they themselves are now revered as saints. Why is this?

A: This is answered by Shah Shuja of Kirman, when he said: 'Great men are great until they know it. Saints are holy until they know it.'

Q: If I feel myself to be ignorant, how can I start to acquire knowledge?

A: The ancient proverb is descriptive of this state: 'Knowledge is in stating ignorance'.

Q: How can one become a Sufi, knowing that one might be losing something in embarking on the way?

A: The Sufi saying corresponding with this question is: 'A poor man fears no thief: a Sufi fears no deprivation'.

Q: Many people who are disturbed seek peace.

A: They may never find it, for it has truly been said: 'Worry is a cloud which rains destruction'.

Q: What is a fundamental mistake of man?

A: To think that he is alive, when he has merely fallen asleep in life's waiting-room.

Q: How can I combine different methods of study, retaining the ones which I have found useful in the past?

A: Just as surely as you seek to find two dawns in one single day.

Q: Must a student always occupy himself with trivialities, as are often mentioned in Sufi writings?

A: There is a saying: 'If you seek small things to do, and do them well, great things will seek you, and demand to be performed.'

Q: Why should one vary one's interests, instead of concentrating only on the spiritual, according to your precepts?

A: This is summarised in the injunction: 'If you have two shirts, sell one and with the money buy a flower'.

Q: I have no idea of what tomorrow might bring, and therefore wish to prepare myself for it.

A: You fear tomorrow: yet yesterday is just as dangerous.

Q: Is speech the best way of communicating?

A: Sometimes, but not always. Hazrat Ali, in a saying attributed to him, says: 'Man is in disguise, covered by his tongue'; and that refers to such cases.

Q: Can crash programmes of study and investigation not enable us to get to grips with Sufi teaching?

A: Hafiz said: 'Huge buildings and colleges, and colloquia, cloisters and university halls: what is their advantage if the heart is not wise and the seeing eye is absent?'

Q: I have learned much and benefited greatly from what I have studied. What can you comment on this?

A: Jami, in his *Baharistan,* refers to this state when he says: 'Now that I have found thee, I know that in the first step I took, I moved away from thee.'

Q: How can I help myself?

A: By remembering the proverb: 'The Path is not to be found anywhere except in human service', from Saadi.

Q: What is the value of externals?

A: There is value, if you realise at the same time the truth of Saadi's dictum, in the *Bostan:* 'The Path is not in the rosary, the prayer-mat and the robe'

Q: Prudence requires one to look before one leaps.

A: Prudence would require one not to leap at all. Hariri says, in his *Maqamat:* 'Safety is on the river's *bank.*'

Fox and Lion

Q: What is the the first step in 'learning how to learn'?

A: It is undoubtedly to abandon the attempt to learn entirely through one's own assumptions. Most people are trying to learn by means of concepts which they have adopted but have no suspicion that these will not work.

There is a story told by Saadi in his *Bostan,* about people misdiagnosing their capacities and situation.

A man one day saw a limbless fox and wondered how it could keep itself alive, so he decided to watch it. Presently a lion came along with some meat, ate some of it and abandoned the rest. From this the fox made his meal.

The watching man concluded on the basis of this incident that he should do the same, since Providence would surely accord him similar treatment. He waited a long time, but all that happened was that he got weaker and weaker. But eventually a voice said to him: 'Do not behave like a crippled fox! Be like a lion, so that you can obtain something and leave some for others!'

Sufi teaching, unlike that which is followed by others, does not assume that you know how to approach something in order to learn about it. Sufis first make sure that the student approaches the matter in the right way for him.

The Effect of Mystical Knowledge

Q: Why can people not be given the full facts and power of the knowledge which all mystics traditionally allow only a little at a time, and to selected disciples at that?

A: In the words of Ibn Hazm, al-Tahiri, of Cordova:

'Abstruse sciences are like powerful medicines, which cure strong bodies and kill weak organisms. Similarly, abstruse sciences improve the mentation which can understand, and improve its shortcomings. They also kill the weak understanding of some people'.

This 11th century thinker whom I have just quoted*, according to the assessment of Western scholars, is the founder of the science of comparative religion. He wrote the first book on the subject:

Q: When was the second one written?

A: Not for another seven hundred years – which is a useful reminder about the supposed continuity of scholastic activity.

Questioner: I think Ibn Hazm is a fool.

A: I am only quoting him. But let us give him a chance to answer you: do you think that anyone can escape opposition and maledictions?

Q: Yes.

A: Then I quote you from Ibn Hazm again: 'Anyone who thinks that one can escape criticism and vituperation is insane!'

Museum-keeping

Q: How can we learn more about the Sufis of ancient times,

*From his *Kitab al Akhlaq wa'l sir fi adawat al Nufus* (short title: 'Behaviour and Medication of Souls').

before the classical period when all the major Sufi classics were written, and were those not equally important times and people?

A: In *Fihi ma Fihi* (In it what is in it), Rumi deals with one of these points when he says that, although a shadow might enter a house before a man, it is effectively not the shadow which is more important and if you are not concerned with shadows and are concerned with men, the man may be said to have entered first. So first we should ask what the purpose of the question really is.

If you are hungry or in need of nutrition, you may ask me about a fossilized banana-skin on the ground. If I have, or have knowledge of, a fresh banana, what is the purpose of the discussion along the lines which you have initiated? If you were not hungry and were a museum-keeper, there might be some point in the question. There still might be little point in asking me, if I were concerned only with fresh bananas. It would help us both if you could decide what your function is in the situation.

This point has sometimes been answered by people to the effect that they want both to eat bananas, as it were, and also to look at the fossils. If we had ever found anyone who was capable of both, the remark might be more productive of further discussion. Remember the man who said that he wanted 'wetter water'. He might have wanted it, but he did not get it. And if he had got it, would it have benefited him, since his organism was perfectly well suited to conventional water?

Subjective Behaviour

Q: *Why do Sufi teachers display behaviour which seems at variance with that of people of insight and of holiness?*

A: One might as well ask why dictionaries have so many words with conflicting meanings in them. Here is a classical instance of teaching through behaviour:

STOLEN RAISIN

Abu-Uthman relates* that he was once with Abu-Hafs, who had with him some raisins. Abu-Uthman took up a single raisin and placed it in his mouth. The other man seized him by the throat, crying out:

*In Kalabadhi's *Kitab al-Taaruf.*

'Thief, why are you eating my raisin?'

Abu-Uthman explained:

'I believed in your freedom from attachment to things of the world, and I knew of your unselfishness, so I took a raisin.'

Abu-Hafs said:

'Idiotic man! You are trusting me while I cannot trust myself (to be unselfish).'

Abu-Hafs was demonstrating that one cannot rely upon reputation, but must develop to the point of perceiving inwardly what the real state of another individual is.

Cause and Effect

Q: Why is my life so miserable? I am often in despair, and then things seem to happen to me to make me even more worried. I feel that other people do not have anything like the problems which beset me.

A: Anyone who had your attitude would probably have similar problems to yours. Has it not occurred to you that, conversely, other people do not have your difficulties because they do not react as you do to what happens?

Have you heard the account of the experience of Farisi and the snake?

THIRST AND SNAKE

The Sufi Kalabadhi was told by Farisi:*

'I was going through the desert when I became so thirsty that I could not walk. I sat down and, recalling that it had been said that just before someone dies of thirst, the eyes start to water, I waited for this to happen.

All at once I heard a sound and saw a silvery white snake slithering towards me. I was so frightened that I leapt up and fled, in spite of my feebleness, with the snake just behind, hissing as it went.

Eventually I arrived at a place where there was water, and I could not hear the snake hiss. When I looked back, I saw that the serpent had disappeared. I drank, and my life was saved'.

*Abu'l-Hasan al-Farisi, in Abu-Bakr al-Kalabadhi's *Kitab al-Taaruf*.

37

Farisi, when he sat down, was not helpless, although he thought he was until the snake approached. And the snake, the second calamity, was the means of his deliverance.

Attraction and Importance

Q: The great Sufi Bayazid is reported to have said: 'All that I desire is that I shall have no desire'. This looks like the kind of 'mystical' remark which Eastern thinkers are famous for making. Does it mean anything at all? If it does, what is the meaning?

A: Desire means, for ordinary people, wanting something, and it is always concerned with selfishness, however much concealed or socially sanctioned. It has often been noted, for instance, that people who seem to be altruistic are in fact obtaining satisfactions from this posture. Now, according to the Sufis, you cannot be paid twice for the same thing. In this context, this statement means that if you desire something and take pleasure in feeling that desire, you have been paid. Even if you are deeply emotionally stirred in what seems to be an other than pleasant way from desiring, you are still being 'paid' by the emotional stimulus.

The Sufis also hold that desire of this kind holds people back: they obtain satisfactions or feed their desire until they are either satisfied or chronically dissatisfied. But, they continue, beyond this there is a way of progress, understanding, perception, which is 'veiled' (obscured) by desire. For this reason, Bayazid seeks the avoidance of desire.

Mundane things, and this includes emotional stimuli which are often imagined by very devout people to be religious, are pursued by means of this desire, this coveting. It is evidenced by the fact that the thing desired acquires a great importance in the mind of the victim, rather as one desires possessions, importance, recognition, honours, successes. To distinguish real objectives from secondary ones the Sufis have said: 'The importance of something is in inverse proportion to its attractiveness.' This is the parallel of the negligence with which people often fail, in the ordinary world, to recognise important events, inventions or discoveries. That this is appreciated in day-to-day matters is perhaps evidenced by the appearance of this statement in a London daily newspaper recently* as 'The importance of a subject can be judged by the lack of interest in it.'

* *Daily Mail*, 17 March 1979, p. 7 col. 4, quoting P. Butler, of Sussex.

3

SUFI STORIES

Rich and Poor

The great lawgiver Moses was on his way to see God, to ask for guidance about his future work.

On the way he met a mendicant, who said:

'Where are you going, Moses?'

Said the prophet:

'I am on my way to see God.'

'When you see him, will you say that I am poor and that I do not know what to do to improve my condition?'

Moses undertook to ask.

Presently he came upon a very rich man, who asked:

'Where are you going, Moses?'

'To see God.'

'When you do, will you ask him what I am to do? I have too much money, and still he showers it upon me.'

Moses agreed to ask.

Eventually, Moses met God, and said:

'Lord! I have come to ask how I should carry on the work. And I have to ask for advice about two men whom I met on the way.'

He told God about the rich man and the poor man.

God said:

'O Moses! You ask me to tell you how to continue with your work. But in the cases of the rich and the poor men you did not do what you already knew was equitable: giving to the poor one the excess of the rich one. How can I tell you to do more, when you do not do what you are supposed to be doing already?'

Played Upon

Generosity of mind, which is so often represented as a virtue, is in one sense the highest form of selfishness: in the sense, that is, that it enables people to reach heights denied to the miserly and small-minded.

Fear of loss and exulting at gain are methods of emotional stimulus which both provide temporary excitement (which people crave) and stand in the way of deeper understanding.

Most people are played upon by others, by their own ideas, by the environment, to such an extent that they are often unaware that there is any range of experience which is separable from these superficialities.

The Persian poet Liwai has illustrated this in his rendering of a traditional tale which is both enjoyable and instructive:

There was once a rich man sitting by the wayside to picnic on his way home from a long journey. He was enjoying his food, thinking of his profits, and contemplating with pleasure the moment when he would reach his house.

As he ate, a traveller came from the opposite direction. The merchant saluted him, and asked how things were in his town.

'All is well.'

'Do you know my house? How are my wife and son?'

'Yes, your son is well, and his mother is flourishing.'

'What of my camel?'

'Contented and healthy.'

'And is my dog on guard?'

'As always, faithful and awaiting you.'

Now with the last possible anxiety lifted from his mind, the merchant began to eat with renewed appetite.

He offered nothing to the other traveller, who thought he might teach him a lesson.

A gazelle ran past, and the traveller sighed deeply.

'What is the matter?' asked the merchant.

'I was just thinking that, had your dog not died, it would have been able to outpace that gazelle!'

'My dog dead? How did it happen?'

'He ate too much of the meat of your camel!'

'My prize camel dead, too? How did that happen?'

'It was killed to provide the meal at the funeral of your wife!'

'My wife! How can she be dead?'

'She died of grief when your son died!'

'My son! What happened to him?'

'He did not survive the collapse of your house!'

At this the merchant rose, tore his robes to shreds, and ran, screaming, into the wilderness.

If the merchant had given the traveller some of his picnic, he might not have had to go through such a harrowing experience as to hear all those false reports. On the other hand, it has been remarked, unless he had been stingy, he would not have had the opportunity of seeing his own behaviour when faced with the traveller's 'news'. But, if he had not been stingy, would he have needed the shock treatment which gave him the chance to observe himself?

The Dervish and his Wish

When human beings were having their characteristics given out to them, one of the angels came to a man who was to be a dervish, and asked, 'What do you want?'

The Dervish-to-be answered 'Nothing', and continued to sit in contemplation of Truth.

Now the Angel went from one to another of the humans-to-be and asked their wishes.

The King-to-be said, 'Pomp and importance'.

The Peasant-to-be said, 'Work to do'.

The Warrior-to-be said, 'Glory'.

And so it went on.

Then a voice said to the Dervish-to-be, 'You have asked nothing for yourself, and it is not too late to choose. Because of your desire for Truth, however, you shall have a glimpse of how humanity will use the attributes....'

As the Dervish-to-be looked into a mirror that was held before him, he saw kings in their pomp and ceremony, peasants working endlessly, soldiers continually fighting....

Then the Dervish-to-be gasped, 'But what will be the future of the People of Learning?'

The picture in the mirror shifted and he saw priests and scholars and experts of all kinds. They had asked for opinions, and for convictions, and for learning. As a result of course, they were often led astray, and they led others just as far away from Truth.

The Dervish-to-be cried out, 'But why is there no way of seeking Knowledge without opinion, Truth without obsession, fact without personal attachment to it?'

'It is somewhat too late for those things to be given to the existing types,' said the Angel, 'and therefore people will now regard facts as knowledge, opinion as enlightenment, commitment as piety and worth.'

'But' said the Dervish-to-be, 'how will people come to know that

45

truth is not opinion, that facts are not knowledge, that belief is not worth?'

'Because', said the Angel, 'when opinion is taken as fact, it does not fit properly. When facts are believed to be knowledge, there is an irregularity in the person who tries to integrate this into himself. When obsession is confused with duty, again it leaves a space.'

'And then what happens?' asked the Dervish-to-be.

'And then, the people who try to fit the one into the place of the other become vain, get angry, are seen to be petty, and people observing them will start to look instead for real knowledge.'

The Dervish-to-be asked, 'But will anything stop people from seeing the shortcomings of the specialists?'

'Only' said the Angel, 'if there is too much vanity, emotion and pettiness on the part of the observer.'

Do as your Friends Wish

A certain Sufi was visiting the city of Samarkand, whose ruler claimed:

'There is no sense or reality in the Sufi allegation of "Truth beyond appearances". One thing which is, however, true, is that people become friends, and friends do as their friends wish.'

'Would your Highness care to name three of your friends?' the Sufi asked.

'Certainly. There is Judge Afifi, Qabil the Hunter and Salim, the Sultan of the Merchants.'

'I can prove that friends do not do what friends want,' said the Sufi, 'but you will have to give me three weeks.'

'Three weeks, but if you do not succeed, your head will roll!' answered the Khan.

Three weeks later, the Sufi called the Khan into a room. Three men sat there, Afifi the Judge, the Hunter Qabil and Salim the Merchant.

'Here,' said the sage, 'is the real situation, contrary to your imaginings. Afifi has sworn to kill Salim, and Salim wants to destroy Afifi. Which one has your support – both? How can you do as your friends wish?'

'And Qabil?' asked the Khan.

'Qabil wants to kill *you*. No doubt, as a good friend, you will help him?'

Hypocrite

Anwar Abbasi relates:
I saw a God-intoxicated dervish sitting by the roadside, covered only with a tattered blanket.

A charitable man, a rich merchant, also seeing him, hurried to his shop and brought back a valuable Kashmir shawl. This he placed gently upon the dervish as he slept, hoping for merit and happy to be of service to the servants of the divine.

As I watched, a number of soldiers of the King approached along the highway, in earnest conversation with a scholar whom they had met on the way.

They saw the sleeping dervish. The scholar gesticulated and the soldiers started to belabour the poor man. They tore the garment from his shoulders and threw it into the nearby stream.

He for his part made no complaint, and I approached him to see what he had to say.

'My friend,' he said, 'do not blame the people of the world if they see a dervish clad in precious robes and fall upon him with imprecations. If they were not typical, there would be no dervishes, shawls, scholars or soldiers in the world. . . .'

The Monster

There is a story of old, once told by a people who hearkened to wisdom. As the members of that community do not now listen to meanings, it really matters little whether they are told the story or not, or have preserved it or not.

But to proceed: the story concerns four men, who lived in the same neighbourhood, and had all studied the theoretical and practical arts to such an extent, and under the greatest masters of knowledge, that everyone was convinced that they had reached the apogee of knowledge.

It so happened that the four came to the conclusion that they should travel and exercise their knowledge, for has it not been said that 'He who has knowledge and does not use it, it is as if he were a fool?'

In short, the friends became wayfarers, seeking opportunities to act upon their knowledge. It also happens to be true, as has been known both before and since, that three of the scholars were deeply versed in arts and sciences, in theory and practice, while the fourth, while less celebrated in customary terms, was well endowed with understanding.

After some days, during which they came to know one another more and more, and when they had had many debates and discussions, the three well-matched scholars felt that their companion was nothing like as well endowed with learning as they, and they tried to make him leave their party to return home. When he refused to do so, they said, 'It is typical of an insensitive one like you, bereft of appreciation of the great capacities which we others have, to persist in representing yourself as our equal.' But they allowed him to accompany them, although they excluded him thenceforth from their important deliberations.

Now it so happened that one day while the four were walking along, they came upon a heap of bones and other remains of an animal, by the roadside.

'Ah,' said the First Scholar, 'I can perceive through my knowledge that this is the carcass of a lion.'

'And I,' said the Second Scholar, 'have the knowledge to reconstitute its body in a viable form.'

'As for me' said the Third Scholar, 'I have the capacity to reanimate things, and I can bestow life upon it.'

They decided to apply their respective powers in these ways.

The Fourth Scholar, however, caught the others by the sleeve, and said:

'I must inform you that although you object to my skills and theoretical abilities, I am yet a man of understanding. This is indeed, as you have perceived, the remains of a lion. Bring it back to life and it will destroy us all if it can!'

But the three other scholars were far too interested in exercising their theories and getting on with their practices. Within a few minutes, the mound of skin and bone was reconstituted into a living, breathing, clearly very dangerous lion.

While the practitioners of learning were busy with their operations, the Fourth Scholar climbed a tall tree. As he watched, the lion fell on his companions and devoured them. Then it roared

48

away into the wilderness: and the only survivor of the expedition came down from his tree, and made his way back to his country.

Asleep and Awake

Once upon a time, in Old Baghdad, there lived a man named Hasan, who was for long contented enough with his lot. He lived a harmonious life, attending to his affairs and looking after his small shop, which his old mother helped him to run.

But, as time passed, he became uncertain as to the drift and direction of his life. 'Is there not more?' he asked himself, and wondered, especially when sitting in contemplation in the evenings, whether he might not experience more and achieve what was possible to him.

Because he gave voice to these thoughts, certain men of religion in his locality were pleased to brand him as a free-thinker and malcontent, saying 'Dissatisfaction is another word for ingratitude, and aspiration is a veiled term for greed; surely Hasan should be denounced by all right-thinking men!'

People listened to the narrow-minded clerics, and were annoyed by Hasan's questionings, and presently he could find few who would bear his company for very long. Even those who would listen to his ideas were confused by them; and Hasan regarded them as shallow people in any case.

So Hasan took to wandering away from his shop and sitting, towards evening, at the cross-roads at the end of his street, to ponder his desires and to think over the hostility of the supposed wise men.

One day it happened that the Caliph Haroun al-Rashid, Commander of the Faithful, was on his nightly rounds in disguise, accompanied by his faithful minister Ja'far and his black executioner, the eunuch Masrur, when they came upon the huddled figure at the cross-roads.

'There must be something of interest to us in this man,' said the Caliph to his companions. To Hasan he said:

'May we spend some time talking with you, as we are travellers who have completed our work in this city, and are without friends?'

'Willingly,' said Hasan, 'and as you are strangers you shall come back to my house, where I can entertain you better than at a cross-roads.'

The four made their way back to Hasan's house, which he had equipped quite luxuriously for the entertainment of guests – though he hardly ever had any – and passed a pleasant evening.

'Friend Hasan' said the disguised Caliph, 'now that we are so well acquainted, tell us something of your desires and of your likes and dislikes, to while away the time....'

'Honourable Sir and kindly traveller' said Hasan, 'I am really a rather simple man. But it is true that I would like one thing, and I dislike one thing. I would like to be Commander of the Faithful, the Caliph himself, and I dislike above all the contemptuous and small-minded self-styled men of religion who make it their business to harass all those who are not as hypocritical as them-selves....'

When an opportunity presented itself, the Caliph slipped a dose of powerful narcotic into Hasan's drink. Within a few moments he was unconscious and the powerful Masrur carried him back to the palace.

When he came to himself, Hasan found that he was dressed in imperial garments, lying on a silken couch, in the palace of the Caliph, with minions massaging his hands and feet.

'Where am I?' he cried.

'In your palace, O Commander of the Believers!' chorused the attendants – for this is what they had been ordered to do by Haroun himself.

At first he could not believe that he could possibly be the Caliph; and Hasan bit his finger to see whether he was still asleep. Then he thought that he must have been bewitched by some genie, some king of the genies, at least. But, little by little, as his orders were carried out and everyone behaved towards him with the very greatest respect, he became convinced that he was, indeed, Haroun Al Rashid.

He gave orders that the corrupt self-styled divines were to be thrashed; that all the pay of the soldiers was to be doubled; that everyone should be exempted from military service, that the River Tigris was to be dammed; that people who wanted to leave the city should be prevented and those who wanted to come in should be stopped ... In fact, such was the effect of his surroundings and the lack of any directing instinct upon him that, had his orders been carried out, the good order of the realm would have been seriously undermined.

The political advisers suggested that he should make alliances; the military commanders requested that he prepare for war: the merchants sent delegations pressing for higher prices; the citizenry petitioned for more liberal administration. The wise men counselled caution and this and that action. Hasan listened to all of them and was influenced now by one and now by another.

And all this happened within the space of a single day, between his waking up in the early morning following the soporific draught and the evening of the same day.

All the time the Caliph and Ja'far and Masrur watched their unwitting guest from a place of concealment which had been specially built for the purpose.

Finally Haroun called his friends together and said:

'This is not the man whom we seek; one who will respond to the opportunities and also the difficulties of power in such a way as to make the most of human life, discharging obligations and carrying on enterprises for the good of all, including himself. Release him!'

So Hasan was again drugged, dressed in his old clothes, and taken to the cross-roads near his home, where he woke up some time later shouting, 'I am the Caliph, and demand that you obey me!'

When he was thoroughly awake, however, he was quite sure that it had all been a dream. From time to time after that, he used to think that that had been quite the most amazing sort of dream, that he had indeed lived in another reality. But he never was able to return to it.

The Greater World

There was once a man who became tired of his life in his village. The more he heard, from travellers passing through the nearby market town, of the 'greater world', the more he longed to enter it, and to escape from the limitations which he felt surrounded him at every turn.

Finally he made his decision, and set off down the road which led away from his village, seeking the Greater World.

Soon he found himself upon a highway with one other traveller on it. They talked, and our friend formed the impression that his companion knew a great deal about this Greater World; so, when he was invited, he agreed to accompany the other man – whom we will call the Sage – on his way.

51

When they had been walking for some time, the Sage said, 'What is that thing by the side of the road, and what could one do about it?'

The traveller looked, and saw that it was a swarm of bees, which was attached to a tree-trunk. He said, 'It is a bee-swarm. I think I'll take it with me. I might be able to sell it.'

So he took off his coat, and using it as a makeshift sack, collected most of the bees and slung the coat over his shoulder. Now some of the bees crawled out of the coat and buzzed about angrily for a time. Then they stung the traveller in the hand. He hopped about in agony and dropped his bundle. Then, picking up the coat, he dashed it against a rock, until all the bees had been detached from it.

The Sage said, 'Let us sit down here and think about this. What have you been doing?'

'Some of the bees stung me, and so I reacted normally.'

'Is it normal to punish all the bees for what some of them did?'

'You know that anyone would have behaved like that!' said the other man, thinking how tedious these philosophers are.

'But what do the bees think?' asked the Sage. He made a mysterious signal, and the traveller saw that there were three or four bees on the ground near where they sat. Through the power of the Sage's signal, he supposed, he could understand what they were saying to one another.

One of the bees said to one of the others, 'Master, as the Wise Bee of the Age, perhaps you can explain to us what has just happened.'

The Wise Bee answered, 'Yes, indeed. Some beings from the Greater World came along and decided to capture us. Some of us stung them, as a reflex action, and one of them then dashed the lot of us onto a rock, in fury!'

One of the others asked him: 'Do they always behave like that?'

'They always behave like that, under similar circumstances' said the Wise Bee; 'but it is because so many members of our swarm wanted to get into the Greater World without knowing anything about it that we were seized in the first place.'

Another of the bees said, 'Well if the Greater World is like that, I for one want to give up my search for it, and no longer consider myself a member of your School, however wise you may be....'

'And you' said the Sage, turning to his companion, 'like the bees, have been trying to enter the Greater World: but as soon as you start on the road, you do something which you regret....'

52

The Lost Jewel

There was once a man who lost his most precious possession, a jewel of inestimable worth. He had been deeply attached to this gem, and was determined to find it if there was any way that this could be done in this life. Making enquiries everywhere, he was led in all directions by soothsayers and false prophets, by astrologers and palmists, by mendicants and magicians. After a long time, when he had still not given up hope, someone suggested that he should ask a certain Sufi, who was reputed to be able to work miracles.

When he had explained his trouble to the Sufi, the wise man said:

'I will resolve your problem, providing that you will do something for me.'

'I shall do anything,' said the excited man.

'Very well,' said the Sufi, 'go and find me, and bring him here, a man who has never lost anything.'

The man asked everyone in his village, then in the nearby town, then in the country; and then he travelled from country to country, asking for a man who had never lost anything. Wherever he went, of course, people not only said that they had lost things, but insisted, more often than not, when reminded of their loss, in telling him what they had lost, and how much it grieved them.

Finally he felt that he had heard of so much pain and loss that he really cared very little for his own trouble. But by now he had become obsessed with finding someone who had had no loss.

After years of this searching, he heard that there was indeed such a man, and he managed to reach him in an inaccessible cave in a mountain.

'Have you ever lost anything?' he asked.

'Never' said the recluse.

'How is that?'

'Because I never had anything.'

'Then you must come with me, because I have been told by such-and-such an eminent Sufi master that I must bring you to him.'

The sage drew a deep breath and sighed.

'What was your problem?' he asked.

'To get back my jewel.'

'And did you get it?'

'No, I met so many people over the years who had lost things and suffered that I no longer want the gem back.'

'Then what do you want?'

'To take you back to the Sufi.'

'Why should that matter to you?'

Now the man could not think why, when his problem was solved, what the Sufi had asked should matter any more.

'Furthermore,' said the hermit, 'what makes the Sufi think that I will want to go back with you to him?'

'That's right', said the other man, 'that proves that the Sufi did not know what he was talking about.'

'Are you worrying about taking me back to the Sufi now?' asked the hermit.

'Not at all.'

'Then was the Sufi not wise, having engineered this whole series of experiences?'

'No,' said the man, 'if anyone, *I* was wise: for it was I who started to look for my gem.'

And, of course, he never became wise: but he had not wanted to, in the first place.

The Magician's Dinner

There was once a magician who built a house near a large and prosperous village.

One day he invited all the people of the village to dinner. 'Before we eat,' he said, 'we have some entertainments.'

Everyone was pleased, and the Magician provided a first-class conjuring show, with rabbits coming out of hats, flags appearing from nowhere, and one thing turning into another. The people were delighted.

Then the Magician asked: 'Would you like dinner now, or more entertainments?'

Everyone called for entertainments, for they had never seen anything like it before; at home there was food, but never such excitement as this.

So the Magician changed himself into a pigeon, then into a hawk, and finally into a dragon. The people went wild with excitement.

He asked them again, and they wanted more. And they got it.

Then he asked them if they wanted to eat, and they said that they did.

So the Magician made them feel that they were eating, diverting their attention with a number of tricks, through his magical powers.

The imaginary eating and entertainments went on all night. When it was dawn, some of the people said, 'We must go to work.'

So the Magician made those people imagine that they went home, got ready for work, and actually did a day's work.

In short, whenever anyone said that he had to do something, the Magician made him think first that he was going to do it, then, that he had done it and finally that he had come back to the Magician's house.

Finally the Magician had woven such spells over the people of the village that they worked only for him while they thought that they were carrying on with their ordinary lives. Whenever they felt a little restless he made them think that they were back at dinner at his house, and this gave them pleasure and made them forget.

And what happened to the Magician and the people, in the end?

Do you know, I cannot tell you, because he is still busily doing it, and the people are still largely under his spell.

The Astrologers

There was once a king who had succeeded to the throne and decided that he should now be crowned. When the question of the date was being discussed at Court, the astrologers stepped forward and said: 'The date must be fixed only after the horoscope for the event has been cast. When an event takes place without a horoscope, it may be unlucky.'

'Very well,' said the King.

Then a Sufi stood up. 'Your Majesty,' he said, 'according to that doctrine, surely a horoscope must first be cast for the moment at which the coronation's own horoscope is to be cast. Otherwise perhaps the astrologers might do their work at an unlucky moment.'

'Is that true?' the King asked the astrologers.

'Yes, it might be true' they admitted.

'But' said the Sufi, 'what about the horoscope of the horoscope of the coronation. How is that to be done?'

Since, after considerable wrangling, nobody could answer that question, the astrologers decided to change the rules, so that they could get on with their work. And so the King did get crowned in the end.

In the Desert

Handed down from remote times is a story of the man of the desert and his quest, which was carried into the towns and villages and has led to Sufi understanding: even when it is related in conditions very different from those in which it is said to have originated.

It is the Tale of

THE SAINT AND THE HAWK

A desert huntsman came upon a contemplative, sitting in the sandy waste, with his hand on his staff and his arm around a wild-looking hawk, which nestled close to him.

The hunter said:

'How can it be that a man such as you, dedicated to matters of the World Beyond, can hold such a thing as a predator, and a trivial thing like a bird, of any account?'

The wise man answered:

'Answer me one question, and your answer shall be the same as my answer. How is it that you can carry at your side such a killing-knife as you have there, when you must have concern for your fellow-creature?'

The hunter said:

'This knife is here to defend myself against the wickedness of desert lions, which have more than once leapt upon me from a thicket, and only through its instrumentality have I been able to survive and to live until this moment so that I can answer your question.'

The saint told him.

'If I spent all my time in contemplation and none in comforting God's creatures, or if you sought desert lions to kill, you might think me a saint, though I would become incapable of anything else, so that the higher impulses would not reach me. And if you hunted lions from morning to night, people would call you a brave hunter, though this dedication would render you incapable of anything else. You on your part would become unable to experience things of the world. I would become incapable of experiencing the other world.'

4

MASTER AND DISCIPLE

Answers

A group of people who suffered from what is called 'confined thinking' approached a Sufi. They asked him:

'Why do you never answer questions in a simple and lucid manner, as we have been trained to do?'

He said:

'Because my work is to transmit what I have to transmit. Anything I say, and much of what I do, must follow that pattern. If instead I fail in my duty and do instead what you are trying to make me do, I become *your* instrument, not the instrument of Truth.'

A passer-by remarked:

'But the last time you were asked that very same question in my presence, your reply was: "Because I do not want to be like *you!*"'

The Sufi raised his head and said:

'If you would only dwell upon the two answers, perhaps you might see that the answers could seem different whereas in reality they possess the same meaning.'

Present and Absent

It is related of one of the great Sufis of Khorasan that he worked for long hours as a brickmaker, and when people offered him money he refused it. He also used to have long talks with people, encouraging them, and then was not to be seen for long periods, sometimes months on end. This confused the people who tried to learn from him.

One day a man whom he had left on his own complained bitterly and asked for an explanation of his conduct, saying, 'If I have failed to understand, tell me, so that I may again take up the Path.' The Sufi said, 'I am afraid that I can say nothing to you

61

about all this.' This man talked to others, and they added their complaints to his, and gradually they began to lose interest in the Sufi, attaching themselves to all manner of frivolous and more exciting things.

Some of them found themselves in the company of a venerable dervish, to whom they confided their disappointment. He said: 'O luckless ones! He was working as a brickmaker because to take your money, raw and vulnerable as you were, would have harmed you, and he took on the harm, preferring to labour stooped in the burning sun for three pence a day. When he left you on your own it was sometimes because his attention, through your own weaknesses, would have inflated you and made you worse. At other times, he forsook you because he had to make supplications to ask that you should not die before he could help you. At others times, he left you alone because people in even greater need than you were to be attended to. You are the kind of people who see all his actions, which are all worthy ones, as faults, because you cannot perceive goodness and reality, and because you think only of the nurturing of the ugliness in your false selves!'

The people were ashamed, and they said: 'Give us permission, O great sage, to return to our master, to make amends to him!'

He answered, 'The permission is easy, and you have it; but the performance is impossible. He is dead, because his Earthly life had to stop the moment you deserted him: when he had nobody to attend him, he had to continue on his journey.'

They said: 'Whence did you gain this insight?'

The sage said: 'I am the solitary remaining disciple of that same master of yours! Only one in a thousand people want to learn. We were, at the outset, one thousand people. The rest of them are not dead, but they – like you – long ago decided that our late Master was insufficient to their needs. The consequence of this addled belief, born of the madness of the world, is that they are all still alive, and now more than proud of themselves, and all of them are flourishing in the world, and all of them are doomed.'

Take Care . . .

There was once a man who wanted to become the disciple of a certain Sufi sheikh. In fact, he was not prepared to travel the path in the correct order of events, being excitable and greedy; he had, in fact, the characteristics which disable the majority of people from completing the Journey.

The Sheikh, however, gave him a chance, since there was a possibility that he might see, through the consequences of his own flaws in action, that he would have to adopt a completely different approach, and become calmer and more considerate.

After some time, however, this disciple became quite frustrated with the Sheikh's putting him into situations where nothing seemed to happen, and he decided that the teacher was therefore useless.

So he cast around for some other teacher, one who would fit in better with his own assumptions about himself. Naturally, he found one. Now this second teacher was nothing less than a maniac who hated the first one. When he had gained the disciple's confidence and inflamed him with promises of secrets and success, he said:

'Now I shall test you. If you pass the test, you will be able to scale the greatest heights of spiritual understanding.'

The disciple begged to be tested, to any extent.

'Very well,' continued the false teacher, 'go and bring me the heart of your first master.'

The disciple, his head completely turned with the wonderful nature, as he imagined it, of the new teacher, went and killed the Sheikh and cut out his heart.

Overcome with excitement, full of greed for secrets and mysical attainment, he was running to the false teacher's house with the heart, when he stumbled and nearly fell.

And then, as if from the severed heart which he was carrying, came the voice of the murdered Sheikh:

'Gently, my son; overcome your carelessness and greed!'

Measurement of Loyalty

A certain Sufi teacher was surrounded by disciples, who crowded his house night and day. His repute was such that odes were written in his honour, from Alexandria to Samarkand, and the greatest nobles of the seven climes asserted that he was the Pole-star of the Age and the greatest teacher of the Earth.

One day, in conversation with the King of Bokhara, the Sufi

said: 'Men have no loyalty, even when they think they have. While, for the maintenance of good social relations, one has to compromise with human adulation, there is really no such thing.'

The King, however, imagined that the Sufi was trying to flatter him by suggesting that people were not really his followers, and he said.

'O Dervish! Vanity, self-seeking and duplicity are marked in the inwardness of courtiers and others who surround temporal kings like me. But in the case of the Sublime Kings of the Cosmos such as you, such people are not to be found. Only the truly devout follow you, for there is no material inducement for them to do so, therefore their expressed devotion must be real.'

The dervish said: 'In this whole city, and amongst all the people who profess attachment to me, and through me to higher things, there are, to my certain knowledge, only one and one-half people who are not fearful or cowardly, if it were to come to a test.'

In order to test this unlikely theory, the King arranged for the Sufi to be arrested for blasphemy and to be marched through the streets under sentence of death, as an example to the people.

When the Sufi was arrested, not a single person in his entourage resisted. Crowds gathered as he was paraded in one street after another, but nobody raised his voice. After several hours one man rushed up to the guards and shouted: 'He is innocent'. Then, in another quarter of the city, a second man went to the court and said: 'Arrest me. *I* am guilty of blasphemy, and what was reported of the Sufi was said by me. He was only quoting *my* words, in order to refute them!'

When the King and the Sufi met privately to discuss the day's events, the Sufi said: 'You see, it is as I predicted. The man who said I was innocent was the half-person who was not cowardly. And the one, single man was he who was prepared to exchange his life for mine!'

Poisoning the Untutored

A certain famous scholar was surprised and pleased when he started to receive, as pupils, batches of disciples from a Sufi whose liberal views were in total contrast to his own. For twenty years nobody else could gain entry to the scholar's lectures, so filled were they with the Sufi's students.

When he had come to the end of his teaching days, the scholar travelled to the Sufi's house. He said: 'All these years, I have been constantly delighted to note that you prize my teachings so highly that you have continuously sent parties of students to me. My lectures have been crowded out for two decades as a result.'

The Sufi said: 'I am glad that you have been satisfied by my actions. For my own part, I am happy that you suspended your campaign against me as soon as my students started to go to you, and did not restart it.'

The scholar, however, wanted to know more. 'But do tell me', he said, 'what made you act as you did? Which of my addresses impressed you most? How did you come to understand my importance and to respect my role?'

The Sufi said: 'Your role was fulfilled, and surely that should be enough for any man.'

'No,' said the scholar, 'it is not enough. Tell me, omitting no detail, what made you decide to send people to me?'

'I ask you a second time, do not press me' said the Sufi.

'I insist,' said the scholar, 'and I shall not cease to press until you have confided the pattern.'

'Well,' said the Sufi, 'something had to be done to prevent the untutored from being poisoned by your prejudices. I had only my pupils to provide. But we did not lose by it: they were able to complete their education by observing how not to think.'

The Promise

The Sufis say that most people for most of their lives are unable to learn deeper things. This is because of the way in which they interpret what others are trying to teach. Two of the weaknesses which again and again manifest themselves are accepting words too literally and interpreting them too superficially.

This story shows the two tendencies: the disciple represents the first, his friend the second:

A dervish said to a disciple:

'Promise me one thing, and I will do anything for you.'

The disciple agreed.

'Now', said the dervish, 'you shall promise never to ask me to do anything for you – then I'll do anything you need!'

One day a friend asked the disciple:

'What are you learning from your dervish teacher?'

The disciple told him:

'He has instructed me never to ask anything from him.'

'That's not a teacher,' said his friend, 'that is a miser!'

Idolatry

Someone said to a Sufi:

'Teach me to pray'.

The Sufi said:

'Not only are you already praying, but a part of your mind is constantly engaged in it.'

The man answered: 'I do not understand you, for I have been unable to pray to God for many months, for some reason.'

The Sufi told him:

'You said "Teach me to pray", you did not mention God. Now, the prayer which you have been engaged in for all this time is prayer towards your neighbours, for you constantly think of what they may think of you. It is permanent prayer to an idol of money, because this is what you want. It is also prayer towards an effigy of safety and another of plenty. When you have so many gods and so much prayer as a permanent part of your being, is it any wonder that you have no room for any other kind of prayer?'

Understanding

A Sufi was asked: 'Which was the most moving, the most instructive, or the most effective experience of your long life?'

He said: 'The one which I shall now relate taught me so much about what I already knew but did not understand, that it is, for me, the lesson of all lessons. Before it, I was one of the "learned ignorant", thought a scholar and thinking myself wise. After it, I was the one who understood.'

'It was when I went to see the great Sage of Chihil-Tan. He was, when I arrived, due to the intrigues of narrow-minded men, surrounded by a howling mob whose minds had been poisoned against him. He stood on his balcony, not answering, but having come out because the crowd were baying like hounds.

'Then one man began to abuse him louder than all the rest, and he did so to such effect that the crowd were first silenced, listening to their jackal-leader, then uncomfortable, aghast at such violence, then – while the sage stood silent still – muttering against the man who had been their spokesman a few minutes before.

'I thought, "Surely this is a miracle, by which God makes his enemies the means of helping his friends. But what will happen to the leader, who is now becoming a scapegoat for the mob?"

'Then, as the mass began to shout their own erstwhile leader down, I saw the Sage of Chihil-Tan strike him a blow. I thought, "He has done an evil thing, that he could not restrain himself at the moment of victory."

'But the crowd melted away, and I wandered off, without visiting the Sage, for I did not know how to think. After an hour or two I saw a poor dervish with a bowl of curds in front of him by the wayside, and sat down when he offered me some of his meal.

'He read my thoughts as I ate, for he said after a few minutes: "Faithless and merciless one! You wonder why the Sage of Chihil-Tan could not keep his temper, and why he struck his tormentor, voiding in your eyes his repute for restraint. Know, O ignorant measurer-of-superficialities, the reality is different from the imagination, because what looks to you like a fact is truly imagination!

'"The Sage hit the man: that is the only fact. His intention, on the contrary, is not a visible fact, but an imagination of your devil's mind! He hit the man to dispel the crowd: for if he had not, in another moment they would have attacked his tormentor. By hitting him, he satisfied the thirst of the mob for visible punishment. The attacker was not hurt, but rather protected from the fury of the mob, who would have torn him apart. So, you see: what looked like an assault, and was in fact a blow, was the means of preserving the attacker.

'"Until you can see these things, and see them in your heart, you will not be one of the elect, and you will play, like a child with nuts and raisins, and this you will call learning, and assessment, and knowledge. But you will not have understanding, and you will remain an animal for ever unless you learn, and learn, and learn."

'But I immediately said: "If this principle were to be adopted then we would refrain from judging by appearances, and all manner of irresponsible things would be done in the name of saintliness, and every villain would thus have a licence to do as he would, and the world would come to an end!"

'The poor dervish looked at me and laughed and then he cried, and then he said: "O brother of bright countenance! Have you not noticed that the world *is* coming to an end, and that the people who believe that they are doing good, and who lack perception and understanding, are the ones who are bringing it to its end? And yet you look not at that, but in fact wish to aid the process! Do not concern yourself with this, but rather develop the understanding of the meaning of events, not the speciality of the scrutiny of appearances!"'

How the World Aids
the Sufi

One of the Masters of the Path was sitting in his assembly one day when a student stepped forward and asked:

'What analogy can there be of the position which the Teacher occupies in this world? What, I mean, is his relationship with worldly events, and is he dependent upon them?'

The Teacher answered:

'The world is there, and so is the Teacher. He is within it and works outside it. It will reject him and also has to help him, because of his unusual quality. This is recorded in the tale of the Young Man Whose Secret Was Not to be Told. It is as follows:

There was once a youth who wanted to serve humanity. Unlike most such people, he did not desire to do this for purposes of vanity; which meant that his service might be accepted, and that he might, indeed, achieve the role which is so badly needed by humankind.

One night he had a dream, and in the dream he was warned that if he set off to try to help people, he would only harm them in the end, for they would oppose him and in so doing would increase their own cruelty. He was told in the dream that he should conceal from everyone until a certain time, that he wanted to be useful. In the meantime he was, however, allowed to say that he had a secret which was not to be told.

The youth told his parents, first, about the secret. They eventually became so annoyed with him that they lost interest in him, and they made little resistance when he decided to leave the house to seek his fortune.

He obtained employment with a stall-holder in the local town for a time, until one day his master heard him say that he had a secret which nobody was to know. 'Tell me' he said, 'or I shall beat you.'

The youth refused, and his master set about him with a stick until a passing merchant rescued him and took him into his employ.

They travelled much and eventually arrived at the capital city of the country. One day the youth mentioned that he had a secret that nobody should know until a certain time. Again the merchant tried to find out what it was, and when his employee would not tell him, he threw him into the street as a disloyal and probably deranged villain. At that exact moment the Prime Minister of the country was passing. His King was dying and, in accordance with the custom of that country, the Minister had to go in disguise into the streets and seek a young man about whom some peculiarity had been divined by the Wise Men of the Court. He would be the next King.

As he stood beside the merchant's house he saw the youth thrown into the street and heard him say, 'I will not tell my secret until due time!'

And this was exactly the phrase which the Royal Seers had instructed the Prime Minister to seek.

He took the young man to the King's death-bed and the King asked him whether he would accept the Crown.

'I will, Your Majesty' said the youth, 'for the Secret is this: that I will not be able to help humanity adequately until I become materially powerful, as King of the country!'

The Loaf of Bread

A Sufi of great wisdom was asked for a parable of the work of the teachers and the nature of the disciples, and he at once answered:

'There was in former times a man who wanted to protect a treasure from a robber, so that he could share it with the deserving of this world. The robber was strong and violent, and the generous man had nothing to help him but, of all things, a talking loaf.

'The robber arrived at the door of the house and threw it open. Just inside, on a small table, sat the Talking Loaf.

'The Loaf said: "Honoured friend, what is your mission, what your intention, what your purpose?"'

'Now the robber, in spite of being uncouth and greedy, was (like most of us) also intensely curious by nature; he was, moreover, quite taken aback by the sight of a loaf which could talk.

'He said to it:

'How do you come to be able to talk, and what can you tell me?'

'The Loaf replied:

'I can talk because I am in this house, which is a magical one. If you come in, you, too, will develop magical powers.'

'That is exactly what I want', said the robber.

'Before you enter,' continued the Loaf, 'you should note that you will have to go through what I have gone through, which is no small matter.'

'And what have you gone through, you, a loaf, that I, an experienced robber, cannot?'

'I do not say you cannot', said the Loaf. 'But I will allude to my experiences, so that you may have choice.'

'Tell me, then', demanded the robber.

'First of all,' said the Loaf, 'I was a plant and grew in a field. Then a part of me became dry, like death, and fell off. It was buried in the cold ground where it lay until it split open. Then it was soaked in water until it was swollen and shoots came out of it. It grew into another plant, and found itself seized and beaten until its husk was separated from its inward part. The inner kernel was beaten into powder, which was mixed with other powder and put away. Then it was taken out, pounded with water and other things until it became sticky and placed in a terrible heat until it became

70

brown – and lo! It was me....'

'When the Loaf looked up after this recital, it saw that the robber had fled, and he could be heard in the distance sobbing with fear.'

The Sufi continued:

'The robber's greed to rob the house is the desire of the disciple before he knows that the treasure is there to be served not to be stolen. The bread is the process of discovering this: but most disciples are not true Seekers, for they flee from truth by imagining other things about the Teaching.'

Intelligence and Obedience

There was once a Sufi teacher who was approached by two men, who begged him to allow them to become his disciples.

He agreed, on the understanding that they were on three months' probation.

For nearly ninety days the Master gave them no tasks, told them no stories, invited them to no meetings.

Then, when their time was nearly up, he called the two into the courtyard of his house, and said:

'I want each one of you to go outside, where there are camels. Each of you is to take the leading-rein of one camel, and to bring it to me, climbing the wall, and making the camel climb the wall.'

The first disciple said:

'Master, it is written that man must exercise his intelligence. My intelligence tells me that what you ask is impossible, and my good sense tells me that you have only asked this in order to test whether I am intelligent or not, and whether I use my common-sense or not.'

'Then,' said the Master, 'you will not attempt to bring the camel over the wall?'

'I shall not' said the disciple, 'I ask forgiveness for appearing to disobey.'

Then the Master turned to the second disciple, and said:

'What is your answer to my request?'

Without a word, the second disciple started to go out of the courtyard, through the gate. The Master followed, motioning to the first disciple to accompany him.

71

When they were all outside the high wall where the camels stood, the second disciple took the leading-rein of one of the beasts and walked it to the outside wall. He then made an attempt to climb the wall, with the camel's rein still in his hand, making encouraging noises to it.

When it was obvious that he could not succeed, the Master said:

'Return this camel to its place and follow me within.'

A few minutes later, when the three men were again standing within the courtyard, the Master said:

'Everyone knows, since the earliest days of humanity, that the Path demands various capacities. These include the use of intelligence and the application of common sense, and also obedience.

'Obedience is as important as intelligence and common sense. Everyone who has ever taught will know that almost everyone will try to use intelligence and common sense in preference to obedience, thus putting these three qualities out of balance. The vast majority of humanity considers that to obey is less important than to think of a way out of a situation. But it is in fact known that none of these things is more important than another, except in the performance. Now we can find men of intelligence anywhere, but where can we find people of obedience?

'The first disciple is dismissed, because he placed too much importance upon intellect. The second is retained, because he did not jump to the obvious conclusion which men tell each other is the best thing to do, and yet which as often as not deprives them of full capacity.'

He turned to the second disciple and asked him why he had tried to do the impossible.

The disciple said:

'I knew that you knew it was impossible, so that there was no harm in obedience, to see where it led. I knew that the easy way out was to say "It is impossible, I shall not attempt it because of common sense", and that only a superficial person would think in that way. Everyone has as much common sense as would be needed to refuse to obey. Therefore I knew that you were testing my obedience and refusal to choose easy options.'

How to Make Them Hear

A dervish, instructing a disciple, said, 'There is only one way to make people hear you. You must know what you are saying, and you must have the necessary conduct for people to hear you....'

The disciple, irritated by the long time which his ancient mentor was taking to give out his wisdom, felt that he had heard enough, and went on his way.

For some years he studied the art of knowing what he was saying, and cultivated the conduct of a good man. People began to respect him, and few left his presence without remarking what a pure soul he was.

One day a young man arrived at the town where he was to make a speech.

The youth kept shouting scandal, and everyone listened to him. Hardly anyone went to the lecture by the dervish's pupil.

So he went back to his old master, now over a hundred years old, and asked him to explain.

'Ah', said the ancient, 'you are the man who did not wait to hear the end of the teaching. You see, you have to be the kind of saint that people want at the time. If they want a real man, they will not go for teaching to a man simply because he looks like a saint. The qualifications for a teacher are not that he has a certain look but that he has a certain effect.'

Hypocrisy

Yahia, son of Iskandar, relates:

'I sat many evenings at the house of Sufi Anwar Ali Jan. People brought him gifts, which he had converted into food and caused to be served each evening before the time of meditation.

'He would not allow anyone to be near him, and sat in the corner with his hand moving from his bowl to his mouth. Many of those who visited him said: "This man is haughty and lacks humility, for he draws himself away from his guests."

'Each evening I moved my place imperceptibly closer to him, until I could see that although he went through the motions of eating, there was no food in his bowl.

73

'At last I could not restrain my curiosity, and I said to him:

'What is the cause of your strange behaviour: why do you pretend to eat, and why do you allow people to claim that you are haughty when you are in fact modest and abstemious, and do not want to upset or shame them, O most excellent of men?'

He answered:

'It is better that they should think that I am lacking in modesty, through observation of externals, than that they should think that I am virtuous, through the mere observation of externals. There can be no greater sin than attributing merit through appearances. To do so insults the presence of the interior and true virtue by imagining that it does not exist to be perceived. Men of externals will judge by externals: but at least they are not polluting internal things.'

Whispering

There was once a Sufi teacher who was approached by one of his disciples.

'Master' he said, 'I am constantly bullied by the other members of the community. They make my life miserable. Unless it is your desire that I should endure this, I would like them to stop it.'

'Nothing easier' said the Sufi; 'all you have to do is to come up to me when we are sitting in contemplation and whisper into my ear. Then I shall whisper into yours.'

No sooner had this happened the first time than the oppressed disciple became the most favoured among the community. After all, was he not allowed to speak to the Master in whispers?

One day, however, one of the more forward of the disciples said: 'Master, may we not hear what you are saying to this fellow-student of ours? After all, we are as docile and intent as he is.'

The Master agreed, and the next time there was an assembly he called the formerly oppressed pupil and said to him, aloud:

'Can you yoke bulging eyes?'

'Yes' said the man.

'Good. What do you earn?'

'Ten.'

'And what do you waste?'

'Five.'

'What happened to the thirty-two?'

'Twenty-nine are at home.'

The other disciples goggled at this, and when they were alone together they disputed loud and long about the inward meaning of the mystical conversation.

Finally, however, their opinions were so diverse that they decided to ask the meaning.

The favoured disciple said:

'It is all quite simple. The Master wanted to show you that you were easily impressed by trivialities, so he whispered to me. You yourselves decided that this was a mark of favour, and you made yourselves treat me well.'

'But what about the cryptic conversation?'

'It had nothing to do with you. I earn ten silver pieces. I "waste five" on my son's education.'

'But the "thirty-two" must surely be people of importance or spiritual merit?'

'The thirty-two are my teeth. I still have twenty-nine, so they may be said to be "still at home" in my mouth.'

'Ah,' said the disciples, 'he is trying to put us off, because the key is probably in the question which we have not asked, that will be the one with the real inner meaning.' They asked the pupil:

'What did the Teacher mean when he asked if you could yoke bulging eyes?'

'Give me a gold piece and I will tell you.' he said.

As soon as he had got the money he answered:

'That was a demonstration that you can yoke bulging eyes: the eyes are yours, bulging with greed; they are yoked by stimulating curiosity, because all trivial minds are manifested by inquisitiveness.'

'What then, should we learn?' they cried, in anguish.

'The teaching is: covetousness, whether in material or spiritual things, leads to pleasure in trivialities. This prevents you from gaining higher understanding and blocks your progress. It can only be dissolved by a demonstration of how trivial your thoughts really are.'

Self-Obsessed

A man went to the dwelling-place of a dervish and said to him:

'I want to discuss my problem with you.'

'And I', said the dervish, 'do not want to discuss it.'

The man was annoyed. 'How can you decide that, when you do not know my problem?'

The dervish smiled. 'Why should you bring a problem to me if I do not know about it, and do not have perceptions greater than others?'

Now the visitor was both confused and anxious. 'Tell me what my problem is, then, and that will convince me' he said.

'O human being!' said the dervish, 'you are almost completely awry. If I show you that I know what is in your mind, I shall divert your attention to "the miraculous", and fail in my duty of Service, as against theatrical performance.'

'Well, then,' said the man, 'give me the solution to the problem, alone, thus fulfilling the requirement of Service.'

'That I have already done' said the dervish.

'But I cannot understand you at all' said the visitor; 'I am not aware that you have given me any solution.'

'Then go on your way, and seek the answer elsewhere.'

For months after that, this man travelled, and he talked to many people, describing his encounter with the dervish.

One day it dawned on him that his problem had been self-centredness, and that the dervish had been pointing this out. This was his real problem, not the one which he had imagined was his. Not long afterwards, in a city distant from the first encounter, he saw the dervish again. He said:

'I have now realized the wisdom of your speech, and I seek to recompense you for your service to me.'

'You have already done so' said the dervish, 'for, in telling everyone of our conversation, you have been helping to teach, though not desirous of doing so, with yourself as the living illustration of ignorance and perplexity, like a man with an arrow stuck in his head which all but he can see, and with a headache which he alone attributes to the difficulties attending deep thought.

'This was your service. But, though in appearance and conviction you were trying to serve yourself, you were in reality serving wisdom, as I have indicated. In consequence, wisdom has partly manifested, to enable you to see yourself a little better.

'You have, however, served not only wisdom, but also self-obsession, not yourself. In fact, anyone can make you serve anyone or anything, by the simple method of convincing you that you are serving yourself if you take a course of action which is in fact designed to serve some other end. Who is the gainer from such a transaction?'

Alternative View

A certain Sufi agreed to take an ordinary man on a journey to see life and death from another point of view.

They came to a tomb of a holy man around which people were walking and saying prayers. The ordinary man said: 'See how the memory of that man is blessed by these multitudes who circumambulate his resting-place, day and night!'

'The reality' said the Sufi, 'is that that saint is revered because he spent all his time with people, so that they did nothing in this world, and he allowed them to crowd around him and ask him questions until he died of fatigue, cutting off his possible usefulness in other ways and places in the world.'

Next they came to the palace of a man who was waited on hand and foot by people who sang his praises night and day. 'Let us shun this man,' said the ordinary man, 'for since he allows people to behave in this disgusting manner there must be something unpleasant about him!'

'The reality' said the Sufi, 'is that it is because the like of you shun him, he is at the mercy of fawning idiots. It would be far better to discover for yourself whether he really enjoys this adulation, and, if he does not, to help him by showing those people that they are behaving in the wrong way.'

Then they came to a place where a man was talking to a crowd, and they were listening most attentively. 'What a disciplined and worthy collection of people' said the ordinary man; 'we should surely gain something by associating with them.'

'The reality is,' said the Sufi, 'that these people have formed such a habit of listening that they cannot think or act. It would be better if we were to help them think and act as well as listen, not just become listeners ourselves.'

The ordinary man said to the Sufi:

'But if one cannot judge by the outward, and by one's own inward feelings, what is one to do in the absence of a man of insight who will tell one what to do?'

'I did not say that one cannot judge by the outward at all' said the Sufi. 'But I do say that to imagine that everything which looks the same *is* the same is no basis for learning. The outward may be reliable, and it may not be. The teacher can help you to attain understanding which interprets the outward as well as perceiving the inward. While you seek information through outwardness alone, you will not be seeking understanding. If you want cherries, why do you look for diamonds?'

Disguise

A student travelled to a far country. One day he was invited to the house of a rich man; and he was amazed and disturbed to find, among the pampered guests, his own Sufi teacher, dressed like the leader of a cult. He said, as soon as he could speak to him privately:

'Honoured Sir, what has become of you? This matted hair, these bells and recitations, this grotesque robe ... it is you who taught us to shun such things like the plague.'

'Hush' said the Sufi, 'for it is not "What has become of me", but "what has befallen these people among whom I am working?" Do you not see that if they thought I was not a fraud, they would never even admit me to their company? I realised that they would let me come here if they could laugh at me. Now it is for me to use this advantage to help them understand.'

Follower

A man went to a Sufi and said:

'I wish to become your follower.'

The Sufi asked:

'Would you become the follower of a dog?'

'No' said the man.

'Then you cannot follow our path, for I myself am the follower of a dog, and you should account my master as being greater than me.'

'How' asked the would-be follower, 'can you be the follower of a dog?'

'Because I once saw a dog deal kindly with another one which had surrendered to it.'

The visitor said:

'But you have a regular system of discipleship, a study-centre, people coming and going and treating you with the greatest respect. You have reached a higher stage than looking at how dogs behave.'

'You are describing what you want' said the master. 'You want to enter a teaching with regular rituals, with people showing respect, with a visible study-centre. You do not seek to be a Sufi, you seek to belong to such a community. They are not the same thing.'

'But if I have been attracted by your outward shape, it is your fault, surely, for allowing it to be presented to the world in this way' said the other man.

'What the world makes of it is one thing; what the disciple understands by it is another' said the Sufi. 'If you are seeking ritual, community, music, labour, service as you understand these things, you will be most in need of those who can teach you through other methods. To pander to your outward requirements is not Sufism, though everyone in the world may think so.'

The Ignorant

A certain Sufi was asked:
'Why do you tolerate ill-advised questions?'
He smiled, and said:
'In order to gain for us all the advantages of observing such queries as you have just made!'
Another who was present recited:
'Without the night, who would know of the day? Bitter peaches are spurned, yet it is those which help in the acceptance of the sweet.

'The child endears himself to us by mistakes, and gives a clue to what we should do – just as much as we may admire a prodigy.'

1001 Days

A would-be disciple visited the home of a Sufi teacher.
He was told:
'You must try to answer a question. If you succeed, he will accept you for teaching in three years' time.'

The question was put, and the Seeker puzzled over it until he had the answer.

The teacher's representative took his answer to the master, and returned with the message:

'Your answer is correct. You may now go away for the 1001 days' waiting, after which you will be allowed to return here, to receive the Teaching.'

The applicant was delighted. When he had thanked the other man, he asked:

'What would have happened if I had failed to provide the correct answer?'

'Oh, in that case – you would have been admitted immediately!'

Classical Encounter

The kind of classical encounters familiar to readers from the great Sufi literature of the past still continue, all over the world. Their value both for the participants, for observers and for those who read or hear about them, also goes on in the same way.

I was once talking to a noted theologian of Baghdad and touched on dervishes and their ways. Without troubling to enquire whether I wanted a harangue or not, he launched into a tremendous diatribe. They were frauds, impostors and self-deluded. They wanted people to follow them and to get a fat living for posing and doing nothing else. Their mysteries and so-called psychological processes were nonsense and opposed to Islam in any case. The only good work connected with this repulsive cult was among those few clever and self-sacrificing Moslems who pretended to be Sufis and then steered people attracted to them back into the salvation of Islam. . . .

Not only were the Sufis horrors but he would take me this very instant to somewhere where these foul heathens were even now assembled, and prove their noisesomeness to me without any fear of contradiction, and as a service to truth.

I followed him through the streets to a house where, on his knock, the door opened and a young man led us into the courtyard beyond it, into the presence of a number of unhorrifying-looking people who were sitting, in the evening cool, around the rim of a quiet pool of water. They rose politely when the raging divine approached them, and motioned him to repose himself, with murmurs of welcome.

My companion was not impressed. He started to shout: 'Away with hypocrisy, vanity and greed!' in a very loud voice, startling a collection of white pigeons who rose into the air and wheeled about.

'Away with hypocrisy, vanity and greed!' It started to sound like a litany as he repeated the formula again and again, now jumping up and thrusting his face first, then his extended forefinger, into the faces of the dervishes.

They said nothing at first. Then I became aware that they, too, were repeating the chant: 'Away with hypocrisy, vanity and greed!'

This development so infuriated the alleged man of God that he gave a wild cry, smote the heel of his hand on his forehead and, leaving me sitting there, rushed from the courtyard. I heard his shouting from the street beyond the garden wall, echoing away into the distance.

The seated figures continued to repeat the words of their critic several more times until, becoming lower and lower, the sound died away.

I asked their leader, seated on a sheepskin at the centre of the group, why they should take up the cry of a detractor.

He said: 'The man who came here is a well-known and highly respected theologian and doctor of the Law. Many of the things which he says, though only quotations and not reflecting his own state, are valuable and adequate admonitions. We are all aware that it is necessary to make away with hypocrisy, vanity and greed; and we are of course grateful to those who remind us of it, so that we, too, may concentrate upon this necessity for a space of time.

'So we adopted this man's very good advice, to dwell upon the theme which he brought us. No doubt it will do us good.'

'But,' I said, 'since he thinks that *you* are the hypocrites and miscreants who have to be opposed, and since *he* would not imagine that you are adopting the lesson, and since *he* must have regarded your echoing him as a taunt – what good has all this done *him*?'

One of the other Sufis raised his head. 'If he was trying to do good, he should not have sought any advantage from it. Real good is only that which is done without expectation of reward or fear of punishment if neglected. But if you have really not observed what advantage this theologian obtained, I will tell you. He gained the satisfaction of imaginedly convincing us that we were evil and insusceptible to truth. This, in his own mind, made him for the moment feel that he was in some way good. And since he is ordinarily in great doubt about this, he has to seek out evidence for it and to provoke incidents which will support his flagging faith.'

The Doorways

Told by Nurjan Alibay:
I was carrying a bundle of door-frames down the steps of a college, between the second and third floors. A well-dressed man sitting in one of the rooms opening off the stairway called out to me, and I went into the room to see what he wanted.

'Get those things out of here at once' he said.

I told him that that was exactly what I was doing.

'But', I said, 'I think that they are of importance; see how well made they are, and how they fit, one into the other, for carrying; and how light they are – there must be a dozen here.'

I was admiring them because they had been made by the great teacher Masoumi. I knew his work, had found them in the college, realised that they were not allowed there, and was taking them to a safe place. I intended to inform him that I had them, to save him from being criticised, because I knew that he was absent-minded.

The other man said, 'How can you talk with honeyed words about trivialities, negligible man?'

I said, 'These doorway frames were made by Ustad Masoumi'.

With hardly a pause, he answered:

'Masoumi's work is both symbolic and functional! That he should leave so much of it here is a blessing upon us! I knew that he was here the other week. But I thought that he was visiting a colleague of ours. But ... to think that he was working! And those frames will certainly fit our doors! What wonderful, fairy wood. You had better take them back to the floors above, and leave them there. We can certainly make an exception in the case of Hadrat Masoumi.'

When I next saw Masoumi, I said: 'Your immortality is guaranteed on earth! They value your doors above their souls.'

Masoumi said: 'Nurjan, you know that it was your late Father (Mercy upon him!) who placed his cloak upon my shoulders, to make me accepted as his successor in the Teaching. When he did so he said: "Give this robe to my son Nurjan when he is to succeed you. This day will be when people will think that your door-frames are better than his company."'

I later discovered that the frames were not even ones made by Masoumi. But from that day, with Masoumi's recommendation, I became a respected teacher.

Wishing to be Wise

People often mistake dervishes, who are treading the Sufi path, for Sufis, who have already trodden it.

There is a tale, told by a dervish, which helps to fix this distinction in the mind.

There was once a young man, he related, who sought out a dervish, and asked him: 'I wish to be wise – how can I achieve my wish?'

The Dervish heaved a great sigh and answered:

'There was once a young man, just like you.

'He wished to be wise, and this wish had great strength.

'Suddenly he found himself sitting, as I am, with a youth, like you, seated before him, asking, "How can I be wise?"'

Bound Hand and Foot

A disciple asked a Sufi master:

'It is said that "the World is deceit", and yet again, that "Things of the world help to another World." How can deceit help towards goodness?'

The Sufi drew a deep and cold breath and answered:

'Harmless striped flies remind you of the sting of the wasp and help the fly. Is this deceit? When the predator sees the spots on the butterfly's wing, he imagines that it is the eyes of a tiger looking at him, and he flees: is this deceit? Sometimes, indeed, there is no other way to treat with men than to appear to be something which will make them act in a certain way – for their own benefit.'

'If I could only have an illustration of that,' said the disciple.

'And so you shall,' answered the Sufi. 'Have you not heard the true story of a great sage of former years?'

THE KING AND THE DOCTOR

'He was a doctor, and the king of a certain country called him to treat his ailment. The sage refused. Then the King ordered soldiers to seize the doctor, and to bring him to his presence.

'When they were face to face, the King said, "I have brought you here, bound hand and foot, to treat me, for I am suffering from an unaccountable paralysis. If you cure me, I shall reward you, if you do not, I shall have you beheaded.'

'The doctor said: "Let us be placed, together, in a room from which all other persons have been excluded."

'When they were alone, the sage brought out a knife, and said: "Now I shall take my revenge for the insult of your having treated me with such violence." And he advanced upon the King. Terrified out of his wits, the King leapt up and ran around the room, forgetting his paralysis in his anxiety to escape from the Sufi.

'As he cried for the guards, the Sufi ran to a window and fled. The King was cured by the only method which could have availed. But he nurtured a grievance against the Sufi for many years, such is the peculiarity of men who think that "deceit" is always evil.'

Value of Parables

Q: What is the value of parables in 'learning how to learn'?
A: This one should tell you, by means of itself, what use they are:

MY FATHER'S SON

There was once a Sufi who was approached by a prospective disciple.

The Sufi said to him: 'If I say, "My father's son is not my brother" whom do I mean?'

The disciple could not work it out.

The Sufi told him: 'I mean me, of course! Now you just go back to your village and forget about your desires to be a disciple.'

The man returned home, and the people asked him what he had learnt.

He said: 'If I say, "My father's son is not my brother" – whom do I mean?'

The other villagers chorused: 'You!'

'You're wrong!' he replied, 'my father's son is the Sufi in the next town – he told me so!'

84

Heeding and Unheeding

Two disciples were once talking in a Sufi school.

One said: 'I shall die if our Master persists in ignoring me, as he has done for the past ten years: for I came here to learn, and I feel that I am being prevented.'

The other was equally emphatic: 'I, on the other hand,' he said, 'shall undoubtedly die unless the Master continues to harangue me: for every time he does so I realise my ignorance more deeply and am thus that much further towards wisdom.'

The remaining members of the community eagerly discussed which of them was right, until the Master appeared for the weekly meal.

Now one of the community seated himself between the two and held up his hand to signify that he had a request to make.

'Continue' said the Master.

'I wish to ask that you continue to ignore this man on my left until he dies, and begin to ignore this other one on my right, for the same reason: so that the rest of us may become perceptive of your desires. In this way I hope that we shall learn, as well as being delivered from the tiresomeness of amateur dramatics.'

Disputation

It is related that two students of the Sufi Way were arguing about Man.

The first said: 'Man arrives at Truth by personal effort and research. Beginning with ignorance, he graduates to knowledge.'

The second said: 'Man arrives at Truth only through guidance by expert masters.'

They almost came to blows, and were far from resolving their contentions when a real Sufi happened to pass. The two decided to refer the question to him.

'Pronounce on this issue?' he asked.

'Yes, please' they urged him.

'Very well. Now, has each of you seen two dogs disputing about a bone?'

'We have', they said.

'And have you ever seen the bone itself join in the argument? Think about it.'

5
ANECDOTES AND NARRATIVES

Relevance

Q: One of the most impressive sights I have seen is a mass of people at the burial-place of a saint, with such emotion that I was gripped by it as by a physical force. Now, you say that the Sufis forbid such things. How can you deny the importance of an event like that?

A: Perhaps you have not heard the tale of Mulla Nasrudin, which can be treated as an analogy of your experience and your question?

In case you have not, here it is.

Nasrudin was driving a friend in his car at a spanking pace. Suddenly, glimpsing a signpost, the friend called out:

'Mulla, we're going in the wrong direction!'

'Why don't you ever think of something good? Look, for instance, at the speed we're going at!'

Emotion and Drink

I am being asked to illustrate that the learning process is distinct from its emotionally stimulative content.

There is a story of a teacher who spent much of his salary on alcoholic drink.

When this became known, students deserted him, saying 'We can hardly understand what he says.'

A friend, another scholar, suggested that, as he now had so few pupils, he should give up drinking.

The drunkard replied:

'I work in order to get money for drink. Now you want me to stop drinking so that I can work!'

This is an ancient parable about both teachers and students who 'drink': because they use the teaching/learning situation for individual and group stimulation. Like the teacher in the example, learning may become secondary to their prime motivation, excitement.

Ghalib and Qalib

Not long ago I was listening to a radio interview between the North Country representative of a radio station and a Ukranian immigrant in Britain. The Ukranian, although he had left his country in 1944, had a strong foreign accent, but I could understand everything he said. But the English Northerner's pronunciation was so regional that one could only follow him with difficulty. And yet the Ukranian, who had lived in the North for many years, clearly understood every word.

Classical Persian provides the same sort of contrast, especially when there is any regional ingredient. In a recent discussion with an Iranian professor, I had the daunting experience of finding out not only that he pronounced the letter *q* as *gh*, as most modern Persians do, but that when a certain phrase of Rumi's was recited, he confused a word *qalib* (mould, form) for *ghalib* (overwhelmer). The result of this was that the phrase *Qalib az ma hast na ma az u* which means 'The form/model is from us, we are not from it' was imagined by him to mean 'The conqueror is from/of us, we are not from/of him.' The latter may mean something, but this mistranslation meant that the professor was unable to understand from his hearing of the phrase that it meant 'Mind is not from matter, matter is from mind'. It is this kind of thing which sometimes makes orientalists and others believe that some Sufi poets are not Sufis but social pundits.

The regional problem came into the picture again when I explained that *Qalib* here means 'form'. The professor was apparently unaccustomed to this usage, since – as he said – to him this word means 'mould'. Classical Persian perhaps used this form frequently. But Khurasani Persian (where classical Persian came into being) still understands *Qalib* as mould or form or model. Not only did Rumi come from this area (modern Afghanistan) but his usage would still be understood there. It is something like a frequent statement of the best English being spoken in Inverness, in *Scotland*. What might almost be called tribalism rather surged into my friend when he accused me of using an unfair advantage in knowing various alternative meanings for Classical words, since my linguistic background is the still-living 'classical' speech of Afghanistan. When I said that I had not done it on purpose, he only said: 'I am not convinced.'

Virtually Unknown Principle of Human Organisation: Group Studies Paradox

Tradition avers, and experience verifies, one of the least-known and strangest facts about group studies.

Learning groups collect around an individual or a doctrine, or both. Because virtually all human actions are motivated by greed or fear ('whip or carrot'), these are the mainsprings of all study-groups. But these negative characteristics, although they alone caused the individuals to find, enter and persist in the group, are a distinct barrier to learning. The level of greed and fear, because these emotions disturb the learning and 'digesting' processes, must be reduced to tolerable proportions. It is always hard, and sometimes impossible, to do this without introducing new people who have lower than average levels of these two characteristics. Such people are almost always found in the general population, not mainly interested in the 'spiritual' purpose of the group which their presence can help. The only method of attracting them to the group in order for them to fulfil this function is if they are contacted and interested on an ordinary 'human,' not greed- or fear-based footing.

This is the paradox. This, too, is a real reason for people who are 'magnetised' into an esoteric or spiritual grouping to establish lines into the general population which are in areas and on subjects free from the bias of the group. The extent to which this can be done will determine the future of the group and the interaction of the committed 'groupists' and the members of the general population. Each provides something which the other lacks. Through their interaction a healthy community may form. Neither, on its own, will be able to develop into a more advanced organism.

If members of the group are unable to accept that their progress depends on those whom they often tend to regard as less than élite, they will become a narrow sociological group, with highly attenuated, even lost, potential. If the members of the population at large (the other category in the twofold process being discussed) look askance at the group-minded people, *their* own insularity will increase and their potential even for maintaining their situation will be impaired. The reason for this is that, as with, say, a chemical process, the influence exercised on each element by their having been brought into contact cannot be abolished by failure to sympathise or to continue in contact.

The refusal to accept that there may be merit, or even decisive value, in others outside their ranks can poison the prospects of those who reject this information. Failure to take sufficiently seriously the inherent value of a spiritual group (which has shed the very factors which brought it together in the first place in favour of the real, deeper unifying factor beyond) has a similar adverse effect on the 'outside' or uncommitted scoffer.

Most groups, since they are too strongly rooted in selfishness and hope and fear, and because they are almost never organised by specialists, fail to reach the stage where the transformation already referred to may take place and produce the group which can now be called a learning organism.

How to Learn What is Already Known

Someone says: 'If people need something in the way of knowledge, and if they somehow cannot take advantage of teaching, can they be helped by being given indirect teaching? Or could it even be that this might be the only way to teach such people?'

This is a question asked by someone who has read all my books.

The exact situation, and its answer, is given in *The Way of the Sufi**, in a quotation from al-Ghazzali.

Why, then was the question asked?

Someone else wants to know whether beliefs or experiences can have apparently different meanings according to one's psychological or spiritual stage, and whether this fact may not be the cause

The Way of the Sufi, Penguin edition: p.61;

of seeming contradictions in metaphysical teaching.

This precise question, even to the fact that it is in two parts and that they are in this order, is in the Counsels of Bahaudin, translated by me and reproduced in *Thinkers of the East** – only it is given in the form of an answer, an affirmation.

The questioner has read that book. Why, then, do we get the question?

A third questioner asks whether true mystical teachers may be 'invisible' to some people in the sense that such people cannot realise their worth. They may be mistaken for people engaged in some other enterprise. What they are teaching, and its methods, may be imagined to be some mundane activity, even.

This matter is explained, in almost the very same terms, in the instance of Charkhi and his Uncle, in my *Wisdom of the Idiots**. I have ascertained that our questioner has in fact read that book. How is it, then, that the statement becomes a question?

This does point to a certain common feature of much human behaviour. People hear, read, experience things (such as these pieces of information) and they do not digest them. Subsequently, like certain conditions of physical non-digestion, the material surfaces again. What these three people's minds are really saying by repeating this information in a sort of waking-dream fashion, is 'you have not paid attention to this information – look at it'. But it is really being said to the person himself or herself: not to me. Because, however, of a failure to go back to the literature to find answers to questions, to lay these ghosts of ideas, these people succumb to the compulsion of asking the question from others.

You see this behaviour in children: when they ask questions that they could have answered themselves, with a little thought. In the adult it is a symptom of someone who is not taking the trouble to try to do his own thinking. In the process, of course, he is in fact using the person whom he questions as a substitute for doing this work. Experience shows (which is why I make so much of this) that people who have not troubled themselves to absorb information from readily available sources and who instead continue asking questions from others in this way do not profit from the answers. The reason is that the effort of looking for the answer and registering it is part of the learning process. To apply for an answer, to get it too easily, almost always results in this individual again failing to digest the material.

If someone asks you a question, and you help him to find out for himself, or if a student you send him to a dictionary or research source, you do this because you know that this principle is correct,

---

* *Thinkers of the East*, Penguin edition: p.188 (Eighth Counsel);
  Wisdom of the Idiots, Octagon edition: p.57–8, 'Charkhi and his Uncle'.

not because you weary of telling him. By contributing his own intelligent effort, he learns.

Poor Donkey

Q: I have heard of people who have spent time with Sufis and who have not made progress with them. Leaving the Sufis, they have associated with other spiritual teachers, where they have found happiness. What does this mean?

A: We have heard.... How often have I heard that!

Very well, then: have you heard of a tale by Rumi, describing such a situation as you mention:

There was once a poor ass, who lived with a humble man and worked for him. The ass was underfed, but it was alive. One day the chief of a King's stables took pity on the poor ass and had it brought into his care for a time, so that it might be fed and cared for along with the royal horses.

The poor donkey could not help contrasting its miserable state with the splendid condition of the noble Arab horses of the Sultan. It called upon God, asking why there was such a difference in their respective states.

Not long afterwards, however, came a war. The Arabs were taken away and returned terribly mutilated, with arrows sticking into them and covered with bandages. Some did not return at all.

This sight, of course, was the answer to the ass's question.

You cannot judge anything at all without having the context in which it has its being.

Nail or Screw?

People continually arrive saying that they have studied this and that, and it has not satisfied them. They have worked under so-and-so, but he proved unsuitable – or died – and they went to something else. They thought this and tried that, and (finally, of course, though I don't know how, with such a record, they can

94

expect anyone to believe it) they have arrived at my door.

It is their conviction that all these trials and tribulations, all these problems and false starts, make up a more or less coherent whole: they were all heading towards the same thing. Well, it may be so. In any case it is quite amazing (if they are not rationalising their inefficiency and inability to learn) that something should have so guided them that they won't allow that a single wrong decision was made. Some of them have been badly maimed by their experiences.

As for the others, nobody seems to have told them the old joke:

'There is one way to discover whether you need a nail or a screw in a plank. Drive the nail in. If it splits the wood – you needed a screw!'

Washerwomen

Two scholars were talking. One said: 'You know that Sufi who lives in the next town? My opinion is that he does not visit us because he fears that our superior minds will refute his vanities.'

The other said: 'That may well be so, but I cannot help feeling that he will in fact come here, because he will want to deceive us and gain more converts.'

They decided, through curiosity, to visit him, and so the following week they attended his evening meeting. The Sufi, however, had been forewarned about their conversation.

When the two scholars entered, the Sufi said to them: 'I am glad that you have come to see me, for you may be able to help me with a problem which has been exercising my mind.'

'And what, pray, is that?' they asked.

'Well' said the Sufi, 'I have been wondering about the widow woman who lives in the next street. She does not show herself, and it may be that she is afraid that the sight of her will make us realise that she is trying to attract attention. On the other hand, and this is my problem, I cannot be sure that her absence is calculated to increase our curiosity, and that she is even now planning to emerge: to make us discuss her.'

'What dreadful gossip is this?' spluttered the first scholar; while his companion was too shocked to make any comment at all.

'I cannot see why you take my preoccupations so ill' said the

Sufi, 'because they were specifically planned to accord with washerwomen's minds....'

Knowledgeability of the Audience

Dishonest or self-deluded preachers, propagandists and teachers depend for their success upon the comparative ignorance of their audiences.

Our main problem, however, is the relative 'knowledgeability' of the audience; because they know a few things, selectively taught them, they are compelled to judge us by these things.

So we have to teach basic facts, information, possible points of view, without being able to take them for granted, because these are so lacking.

Sometimes I feel like a garage man told by the owner of a vehicle: 'I want you to get that car started,' and am faced with the unpleasant task of telling him the fact: 'Your trouble is that you have got to learn how to drive.'

What They Are Like

A certain king was confused by the growing number and variety of dervishes in his domain. He called his Council of Ministers and sent them, in deep disguise, among the people of the Sufi philosophy, to study them and to report.

His instructions were: 'Find out what these people are like'.

Disguised as clerics, soldiers, friars, merchants, students and farmers, the members of the Council of Ministers (and a multitude of their agents) spent five years in their investigations.

Each reported separately, in writing, direct to the King.

When he opened the letters, he found that every single one contained the words: 'You ask what these people are like. I have to report that they are not like anyone or anything else in this world.'

Samples

People tend not only to assess unfamiliar things in terms of their own experience, but also in terms of parts of their experience which they imagine must be relevant to the case. They do this because they want to gain something, rather than because they want to know something.

This, indeed, is the main way in which we can assess these people: Do they want to take or do they want to know?

This is illustrated by the anecdote of the Sufi who was approached by a businessman, who wanted to be shown miracles.

'I am a commercial man,' he said. 'And, of course, if I am to accept something, I have to see a sample first. Why should you not show me one of your miracles?'

The Sufi said: 'It is not possible accurately to put what we are doing into commercial terms, but we can approximate to your ideas and still show you that you are greedy, not studious.

'Ours, in your phraseology, is a "non-commodity business". This means that you can have references attesting to the usefulness of our service – but samples, no!'

The Road to Khorasan

There was a time, in the Middle East, when the descendants of the Prophet were hunted down like wild animals, suspected of treason, captured and killed, for no other reason than their ancestry.

A story is told of a relative of ours during that time, who was a Sufi of high repute, and a man whose honour was everywhere respected. Unfortunately, of course, he was of such origins as to arouse the hatred and the active opposition of the authorities of the time.

He decided that it was not for him to go into hiding, and that it would not be suitable for him to flee, as being contrary to the manners of dervishes. So he presented himself to the court of the Caliph.

The Caliph was at first surprised at such a meek surrender; but ultimately he issued a death-warrant, which he handed to the captain of the guard, saying, 'You Sayeds are a funny lot; but if you seek martyrdom, I am glad to grant it.'

The Sayed said: 'I have surrendered myself, thus relieving your men of much trouble in searching for me. Will you in exchange allow me to present myself personally to the executioner?'

The Caliph sent him off, accompanied by a couple of stalwart guards. The party made its way to the huge open caravanserai where the Public Executioner was sitting with his minions around an enormous bonfire.

The Sayed said to the guards: 'Now let me approach the Executioner myself, for it is not fitting that a man of my rank who has surrendered himself should be treated without dignity at such a moment as this.'

The guards agreed, and waited until they had seen the Sayed present himself to the Executioner. Then they withdrew.

The Executioner, recognising his captive, said: 'So, I have a customer tonight, by the order of the Caliph, have I?'

The Sayed threw his Order of Execution into the fire without showing it to the other man. Then he shouted: 'I have come of my own free will, as you see, unescorted. And I have been to the Caliph. And I have thrown the Order into the fire. I may have surrendered, but I refuse to be exiled to Khorasan!'

'You cannot refuse anything!' roared the Executioner. 'I shall not fail to execute my master's desire!'

And, instead of executing the Sayed, he handed him over to the Royal Stables to be given horses and an escort. By the fastest possible relays of animals and guards, he was conveyed from the land of the Arabs to the furthest borders of Khorasan, modern Afghanistan, where he was abandoned – in exile.

Service

At the court of the Khan of Paghman a nobleman asked a humble man (whom he envied because the Khan had honoured him):

'Is it traditional in your family to serve illustrious rulers, or are you the first of your line to enjoy this distinction?'

The man replied:

'My ancestors were men of honour; they did not have such lowly aspirations as to desire the companionship of monarchs.'

The nobleman persisted:

'Our Khans are Sharifs (descendants of the Prophet) and Sufis. Do your people not feel honoured, as we do, by the mere opportunity to serve the elect?'

The humble man said:

'Our family have hitherto not had such high aspirations. I am the first of my line to have the temerity to hope to serve such people.'

As Rich as You . . .

One of the nineteenth-century Nawabs of Sardhana was showing his horses to a visitor when the man said:

'I wish I was as rich as you!'

Although he was a foreigner, and therefore not aware of the code of the Sayeds, the Nawab, when he left, presented him with presents constituting his entire fortune. Years were to pass before the estate was able to recover from this single act of generosity.

Someone said to the Nawab:

'Did you have to adopt such a reckless course?'

He said:

'To be false to my traditions would have been impossible. Someone asked today why we bother ourselves to try to impart Sufi learning to the unworthy. It is because they ask us. Do you not know the story of our illustrious ancestor, Ali, the son-in-law of the Prophet?

'In battle, Ali shattered the sword of an enemy warrior, who stood helpless, waiting to be cut down, but at the same time shouting in his fury: "Give me a sword and I will destroy you!"

'Ali handed him his own sword, leaving himself without any means of defence. His enemy, when he had recovered from his surprise, asked:

"How can you hand your only sword, in the middle of a battle, to

99

the man who hates you and is trying to destroy you?"

'Ali said:

"It is the family tradition that nobody asks one of us for something in vain."

'We only know this story today because that same man refused to kill a man like Ali.'

A Word can be One of Three Things...

One of my choicest memories is when I translated into Persian a couplet from Hafiz. It had been quoted in English by a distinguished English judge whom an associate and I were consulting about something. The judge said: 'These lines have always impressed me by their clarity: put them into Persian again for your friend.'

The Afghan Sufi who had just arrived in England was quite amazed.

'Do you say that this man is a judge?' he asked me.

I said that he was, and that he had also taught law.

'Ask him if there is any more in these lines than the sentiments which he admires' said the fascinated Sufi.

No, there was no more, said the legist.

The Sufi now quoted a tale from Rumi:

'A word,' said a grammarian to a dervish, 'can be only one of three things.' The dervish at once started to howl and rend his garments. When he had calmed himself a little, he exclaimed:

'And to think that I had always hoped that there might be another thing than those!'

His Honour, as soon as the story was finished, seemed slightly restless. 'What did you say His Excellency was?'

'Master of the Royal Afghan Mint, in Kabul,' I told him.

'Oh, I see.... One of these complicated customers, what?'

Croaker

*Q: If, as you say, rituals are fossilized exercises, and that litera-
ture or practices outlive their usefulness, how do you explain why
they are so tenaciously held by so many people? They must fulfil a
function which is valuable, surely....*

A: If people want something, it does not mean that the thing is
good for them, or even that it is fulfilling a function which is in
fact useful or irreplaceable.

There is a story about this, which has been found to be a very
good remedy against trying to get something useful out of something useless, even harmful.

There was once a townee who went to a food stall to buy a flap of
bread with watercress in it, which was being sold by a country-
man. As he put the bread to his mouth, a frog leapt out and
squatted on the ground. The townsman, who had never seen a frog
before, bent down and picked it up. The frog croaked, *'Ghar-ghar!'*

'Ghar or no *ghar'* said the townsman, 'you are going back into
this bread. I paid good money for you, after all!'

Wealth of Satisfactions

*Q: What is wrong with following one – or even several – of the
spiritual paths which are so richly available and which offer such a
wealth of satisfactions, as we know by experience of them?*

A: Wealth and riches, the terms you use, constitute a good
introduction to the parable which answers this question:

There was once a miser who put all his money, as it came in
from his shop, into a cavity between the wall of his house and that
of his neighbour, coin by coin, through a small hole which he had
made for the purpose.

This practice even increased his greed, and he craved even
richer satisfactions until he not only spent nothing at all but contrived to visit his neighbour at èvery meal-time, so that he could
eat free of all cost to himself. 'I am, after all,' he told himself,
'repaying him by means of my company: and, anyway, he likes to
be charitable and to feed whomever is in his house when meals are
served.'

101

He even sold his business, and put all the proceeds into the wall, deriving great pleasure from his generous friend's never-ending hospitality.

When, after many years, the man next door died, the miser broke into his hoard, to find that the neighbour had robbed it: he had been eating his own money. . . .

So ask yourself whether the 'wealth of satisfactions' which you can obtain from a spiritual path (or from another source of stimulus) is in any way of the nature of the miser's. . . .

The More the Better

Q: *Sufi teachers often say that you should not do spiritual exercises on your own. They also say that teachers who make everyone do the same exercise are ignorant, and can even cause harm. Why is this, since doing such exercises is a part of all devotional systems?*

A.   In the first place, it is not a part of all devotional systems. It is a part of all systems at the stage when they have deteriorated from correct application of exercises to automatism. Even the 'teachers' do not know this. As to the reason, Sufis don't allow it because it does cause harm, obsession and imagination instead of enlightenment. But you cannot know this until you have experienced the alternative. You will have to rely upon correct information and listen to a tale about it:

There was once a mosquito who decided to kill a proud horse. She said to the horse: 'If anyone could kill you, the most powerful beast anywhere, would such an individual be even greater than you?'

The horse answered: 'Certainly. But, of course, there is no way of killing *me!*'

Then the mosquito stung him. But this was nothing but a pinprick to the horse. The mosquito was ambitious, but could not think what next to do. 'I'll go to the hare' she said to herself, 'because he is wise and people say that he knows how to help one attain his desire.'

The hare, when questioned, said: 'Band all your mosquitos together, act in unison, sting again and again, and you are bound to succeed.'

So the insect called all her friends, and they listened to the wise

102

words of the hare, and were inspired to attain this desire of overcoming the horse. They set out in an enormous swarm, found the horse, and stung him to death.

Naturally, the mosquitos were delighted at their success. They went back to the hare and told him, and all the other animals surrounding the hare at his daily court were equally impressed, and many enrolled themselves as his disciples. Nobody, of course, thought to ask what had been achieved in reality.

Now each of the mosquitos imagined himself to be a champion. They dispersed in all directions and stung everything in sight. From that day to this they have never managed to kill anything by means of their stings alone. Now and again a cloud of mosquitos kills some animal, and this keeps the legend alive, in some circles, that there is something to be gained by stinging, and that the mosquito is the greatest thing in creation – after the hare, which advised it in the first place.

Who is at Fault?

Q: I have been studying under (a certain person) and I am disenchanted with him. His obsessions and those of his followers cause me pain. What should I do?

A: What you should do depends upon what you are like. There may be nothing which you can do. There is a story of a thief who robbed a man of a number of coins. When he tried to buy something with them, they were found to be counterfeit. As he was being led to the scaffold after conviction for trying to pass false coin, he saw the man whom he had robbed, and called out that he was the cause of his ruin.

This has given rise to the proverb: 'Do not steal, if you do not want to be hanged.'

You cannot just choose one event in a succession of happenings and claim redress on that basis.

Pleasant and Unpleasant

Q: 'Why do Sufis often make people uncomfortable, or even hostile, by what they say and do?'

A: If you are a surgeon lancing a boil, and it hurts, does the patient say, 'Why am I being made uncomfortable?' or 'What is being done is a means to an end'?

Q: But if Sufis are releasing the 'pus of the mind', why do they so often give pleasure?

A: If a doctor puts you on a delicious diet, do you then say, 'Why have I been prescribed such delicious apricots?' You know that it is because they contain a nutrition or remedy which you need. The pleasant or unpleasant taste, the experience, is incidental.

6
IN WESTERN GARB...

Sufis in the West

Q: Surely your importation into the West of Oriental ideas, through Sufi thought and literature, must be seen only as the invasion of a foreign system, like the recent introduction of Hindu, Buddhist and Chinese ones, and nothing of permanent influence? If the Sufi forms and concepts indeed had the power to penetrate Western thought, surely they would have done so long ago?

A: I do not know what you mean by 'long ago'. It is true, according to the Oxford English Dictionary, that the word 'Dervish' appears in the language only in 1585, the word 'Fakir' (originally Arabic for the Persian 'Dervish') as late as 1609, and the term 'Sufi' came here in 1653. 'Sufism' itself is first found in the nineteenth century. This currency, however, is already far earlier than many of the intellectual and other concepts which are in the mainstream of Western thought. And earlier than recent 'Oriental' imports.

But we have hardly started. Ghazzali (died 1111) the great Sufi of Iran, was so influential with the European (including English) Medieval thinkers that he was actually imagined to be an eminent Christian theologian; while Roger Bacon was teaching Sufi ideas at the University of Oxford soon after its foundation. The Franciscans, Dante, Chaucer and many of the Western mystics of many centuries ago have been shown by European scholars themselves to have depended upon Sufi materials. In some cases they actually copied from Sufi textbooks.

I do not think that there is any parallel to this ancient presence of historical Sufism in the West in any of the 'Oriental' systems you mention. We build on that foundation, plus the present state of Western society and thought. What the 'Orientals' are doing, it is up to them to display and assert.

As for my introducing Sufi ideas, you should remember that there is an astonishingly large number of books and monographs studying Sufism, entirely prepared by Western scholars, centuries before I brought these materials to the West. My activity is not introduction, but explanation and updating.

Sufi activity, it could be claimed, has been rooted in the West for longer than most ideas which are said to be 'Western'.

Reasons

Q: What is the reason for the way in which your materials are projected in print? I mean, why do you translate some material, represent other portions, use Eastern similes in some and Western psychological terminology and insights in others?

A: There are two criteria: (1) What materials have to be projected at the present time to have the maximum useful effect, and (2) who can absorb them and in what format?

Sufic materials are always presented in accordance with the possibilities. This is because Sufism is not archaeology or hagiography (however much it may resemble them to those who look no further) but effect. Eastern similes which are still viable both in the East and West are used because of this viability. Superseded materials are not regurgitated just because they have been used in former times. Materials are re-presented if this can be usefully done. 'Western' psychological terminology and insights are useful, so they are used.

Look at the results. The published materials are read and accepted in both the East and West; by scientists as well as theologians, by ordinary readers in addition to specialists of all kinds. In a word, the presentation is effective.

If there were no originating impulse from which the material comes and which indicates how it may be used, we would be forced to present Sufi materials like you would any other dead corpus of lore: you would rearrange, prune and present in accordance with subjective assessments. We do not have to do this, since the material itself provides the guidance to those who can descry it. The question, however, illustrates the mind of the questioner more than anything else; for it presupposes that Sufi materials are like those of any other pursuit, capable of being manipulated by rule or whim. Had the questioner taken into consideration the Sufi fact that the Teaching determines its method of presentation, he would not have needed to ask the question.

Folk-Memory

Q: Traditions die hard, and folk-memory retains many truths which are not known by scholars. Is it not worth investigating the psychological and mystical procedures of supposedly primitive peoples, for forgotten knowledge?

A: First, forgotten by whom? I am not aware of any 'psychological and mystical' knowledge being needed and hence sought for retrieval from anyone until the existing materials have been used. Your question is the same as the old one about inventing the wheel. Someone who knows nothing about the wheel may start to question whether there is perhaps not such a tradition in some primitive region. But has he (or she) asked the engineers if they ever heard of it?

Secondly, folk-knowledge is two sided. Some of it is supposed to go back thousands of years. Very well. Now look at this:

'The problem is who or what the clock, which is over 50 years old, commemorates. One group of historians are adamant that it was erected in 1916 as a War Memorial, whereas another group assure me it commemorates the discovery of pasteurised milk.'*

In sixty-two years or so, even scholars can't agree why a public clock was put up in Britain.

The third point, of course, is the 'historians'. Who is to do this investigating of the folk-memory? Only people who know what they are looking for, not just another group of scholars who will disagree with one another. Our enterprise is experiental, which means among other things that what is discovered is factual and not susceptible to varying explanations.

'Men are not Rats!'

When Pavlov showed that dogs could be conditioned, one retort of the time was 'Men are not dogs'.

Be that as it may, social and drinking habits among men – in

---

*Quoted by V. Wood, from *Kincardineshire Courier and Advertiser*, and reprinted in *Punch*, London, s.v. 'Country Life', 14 June 1978, p. 969.

the West at any rate – have been shown in the laboratory to resemble the behaviour of rats rather closely.

The psychologist Gaylord Ellison† has demonstrated that when rats are offered alcohol, recreation and food, in circumstances similar to those afforded man, they tend to adopt similar forms of behaviour.

The importance of this study is that it helps to approach the question of whether 'social' and 'cultural' behaviour is in fact derived from the animal side of man.

Within a few days of being put into their 'human-type' setting, the rats developed patterns which mimic those of Western people. They went to the alcohol dispensers, as do Europeans and Americans, at a pre-meal 'cocktail hour.' Concurrently, again as with humans in a similar situation, they combined this with social activity. Although the alcoholic drinks (or water) were available to them, they – like their human counterparts – abstained from drinking until it was time to sleep. As with many people of the Western culture, they had an alcoholic drink before retiring.

From time to time, people in the societies where alcohol is widely used throw parties – drink a lot – and have hangovers. So with the rats. Occasionally the 'bar' became a place for a drinking party: all rats joined in for this open house. As with human beings after a particularly hectic drinking party, the rats spent some days recovering, not touching alcohol and imbibing quantities of water.

Humans say that they drink alcohol to reduce tension, to be sociable, to do business with their fellow-drinkers, to avoid loneliness, and so on. Can it be the same with rats? Hardly. The explanation seems that some social behaviour, at least, is rooted in the animal level of behaviour.

Science

Q: Are you opposed to scientists?

A: No. But I am opposed to scientists not being what they think they are. I once went to a lecture concerned with blood transfusions, attended by a scientific audience, with a Sufi friend. The lecturer spoke disparagingly of the 'lingering folklore beliefs'

†*Newsweek*, New York, May 8, 1978, page 55.

among ordinary people, and how scientists should work against these. My friend requested permission to ask a question. When he was given it, he turned to the audience and asked them how many knew to which blood group they belonged. One-quarter raised their arms. When asked which of them knew their 'astrological sun-sign,' everyone did.

Reality and Imagination

Q: Are people really as stupid as the Sufis make out? If they were, how could society function as well as it does? How can one test whether people really do behave in such an absurd manner as some of the people in Sufi stories and teaching narratives do?

A: People really are as stupid as the Sufis make out. Society works as well as it does because not everyone is stupid all the time. The Sufi enterprise helps them by showing up stupidity to forestall its appearance at times when it blocks understanding. There is little need to test whether people really do behave as the ones in stories and narratives, because the newspapers are full of accounts of this behaviour, and hence it is displayed everywhere all the time. You do not need, after all, to 'test' whether a cherry is red – you can see it easily, once you know what red is.

There are, however, many people who like for one reason or another to demonstrate human stupidity. Jaroslav Hasek (author of *The Good Soldier Schweik*) was one of these. He wrote an article in a zoological journal, which was highly thought of, asserting that elephants liked recorded music while tigers did not. When he published a treatise on prehistoric fossilized fleas, it was such a success that many European learned journals reprinted it. When he advertised 'thoroughbred werewolves' for sale, he was inundated with orders for them. He put on a police uniform and told the Rector of a Prague Academy that he was under arrest, whereupon the man obediently followed him to a police station.

By these means Hasek showed that people will obey the symbols of authority, that they accept what is written in academic journals, that they will accept even 'werewolves' if they are offered them, that they will publish tripe at the drop of a hat.

And may I ask *you* a question? If people were not as stupid as they are made out to be, would they tolerate the kinds of individuals and organisations which exploit them? Who votes for the lying and improbable politicians who, remember, actually rule over so many of us?

Confusion of Superficial and Perceptive

Q: The appreciation of art must surely be a higher-perceptive function? When Sufis speak of the secondary self, which is composed mainly of the emotional and the learnt, do they not use the artistic sense to break through that barrier, testifying as it does to images and values far beyond the superficial? Surely everyone is agreed that artistic perception is on a much higher level than lower ones?

A: Theoretically this seems to be true. The Sufis say, however, that what most people take to be art is not art at all, but emotional and conditioned sources of stimuli. This does not mean that there is no real art. It does mean that Sufis hold that even acceptedly aesthetic people have confused learnt and automatic responses with perception.

Q: This sounds very much like a posture to me. After all, how can Sufis establish that art experts are superficial?

A: Sufis do not have to establish it, as it has already been established by the art experts themselves. You will recall (in my *Learning how to Learn*) how a man who wanted to get rid of the crowd around Van Gogh's pictures carved something out of corned beef and mounted it as 'Van Gogh's Ear', and by this stratagem attracted the art-lovers away from the paintings. This was a proof that art lovers, among whom were surely *some* experts, were more interested in what was in fact corned beef than in what was acceptedly art.

But if you want a further example, there is the one of 'Sunset over the Adriatic', exhibited in 1910 at the Salon des Indépendants, painted by Boronali. An Austrian collector bought the canvas, after it had received acclaim by the experts as an outstanding example of the Excessivist School. It was then revealed, by Roland Dorgelès and a group of artists, that the picture had been 'painted' by a donkey, to whose tail a brush had been tied. 'Boronali' was formed by a rearrangement of the letters in the name of Aliboron, the donkey in La Fontaine.

Matisse's painting, 'Le Bateau' was hung for 47 days at the Museum of Modern Art in 1961, when about 120,000 people saw it without realising that it was upside down.

There are many true stories of this kind, which surely go far enough to establish that artistic appreciation and 'higher perception' are not connected in the kind of art which is generally regarded as such. No, what is currently considered to be art does not belong to anything higher than emotion and implanted belief: and this has already been well illustrated, no matter what people may imagine.

I have myself, in a certain artist's studio, witnessed a crowd of distinguished visitors, including eminent critics, rapturous over a bundle of rags which, as the embarrassed master painter confessed, were the pieces of cloth on which he wiped his brushes, and not works of art at all....

So the conclusion seems to be the very reverse of what you believe. It is possible to illustrate that what is thought of as artistic appreciation is superficial; or, at least, is dependent upon unreliable feelings and social pressure. If it were to be held that there is something 'higher' in artistic experience, the onus would be on those who claimed it to show that they have excluded these easily demonstrated subjective reactions.

Real and Unreal

Q: In Learning how to Learn *you write vigorously against such things as dressing up in ridiculous clothes and carrying out absurd exercises, and watching fictional spectacles, plus being fascinated by distorted history. Now, surely, there is a strong interest in reality and in real life, even the most banal forms of these. Surely this is an excellent parallel to help to bring people to an interest in the true reality which lies beyond ordinary reality, and which is the 'most real of all'? What about the people who watch, for instance, documentary programmes on television?*

A: I am glad that you asked that. A taste for reality is certainly a motif of a taste for objective reality; so that comparative reality − ordinary life − is a first step. After that comes the showing that ordinary life is not real but perceived subjectively.

But: people have not yet become as accustomed as you may

imagine to seeking reality. They still seek fantasy much more. I am not against fantasy, but I say that the search for too much fantasy at the expense of reality gives an unbalanced intake.

If there are three concurrent television programmes, which of them will get the largest audiences? The one which features bizarre dress and strange physical actions, the one which presents a human life, or the one which is an emotionally-charged costume drama? What proportion of each will the programmes win?

I will not ask you to guess at the figures, for the result will embarrass you. We have got some figures on this. The Paris newspaper *France Soir* carried out a survey of viewing habits. They held a poll to see which of the following was being watched one night, and in what proportions:

1. 'It's a Knockout' – with a mixture of sport and bizarre dress;
2. An historical costume drama;
3. A documentary about the life of a woman.

Here are the results:
Percentage of viewers watching
  'It's a Knockout' – 33%
  Costume drama – 67%
  Woman's life – NIL.
    Yes, I said nil.

Disreputable

Q: I see that such writers as Norman Cohn, in his book The Pursuit of the Millennium, *ascribe the rise of Christian sects wandering about and proclaiming the direct influence of God, to Sufis and Sufism. He speaks of their debauchery, and habit of eating revolting foodstuffs, and states that they reached Europe and influenced it, from Moslem Spain. This is not the behaviour which most people associate with Sufis.*

A: Cohn says* that Sufism 'seems to have assisted the growth of the Free Spirit in Christian Europe. Certainly every one of the features that characterized Sufism in twelfth-century Spain – even to such details as the particoloured robes – were to be noted as typical of the adepts of the Free Spirit a century or two later.'

*Norman Cohn, *The Pursuit of the Millennium*, London, Paladin, 1972, pp. 151f.

114

All publicly-manifested activities and some others have their imitators. The lunatics who go about in India and the West, aping what they take to be the behaviour of Hindus, influence other people. Are we therefore to say that 'these people represent Hindu influence'? The cannibal who always said grace before eating people because missionaries had taught him to do so should not, surely, be considered without qualification as a Christian or even 'under Christian influence'?

But your point is interesting, because we have a very similar development in the West today. Parallel with an increase in real Sufic activity, there are bands of people roaming the streets and filling the halls, enrolling disciples and generally claiming to be Sufis or pretending to be such. They will, in turn, have many imitators.

But the 'features that characterize' Sufism are not those which can be imitated, so Professor Cohn is being somewhat superficial here. Such cults represent the deterioration of Sufi behaviour. They come about by the interaction between unstable imitators (would-be teachers) and emotion-starved, temporarily insane people, would-be disciples.

What it Really Meant...

Q: Modern science, and contemporary ways of looking at things, have enabled us to solve many mysteries of the past. The written records of the Sufis, admittedly, are often obscure because they are presented in a special way. But surely present-day scholars can decipher them when they know the point of view of the writers?

A: Sufi writings are not all encoded: they depend, as often as not, upon someone having a certain experience before he can really understand them.

And there are problems when you call in the 'experts' as a number of reputable scholars found out with a certain inscription not so long ago. One day a small boy found a stone sticking out from the ground, when he was crossing a field in southern Ireland. One side was smooth, the other had an inscription. This he showed to his local schoolmaster, who sent it to the university. There scholars became excited. One found that it was written in Hebrew, and he translated it as a warning of invaders who were to come.

Another, however, was equally certain that it was inscribed in ancient Norse, and told of a battle against wild men after the writer had been shipwrecked.

That is, until an ordinary student looked at it with the sun shining upon it at an angle. Then the message stood out clearly. It was in English, and no more than a hundred and fifty years old. It said, simply:

'June 1788. Am very drunk again this day.'

You will find this recorded in Frank Edwards's *Stranger than Fiction*, London, 1963 (Pan Books), pages 136 to 137.

Who Can Learn?

Q: Again and again the Sufis claim that people do not register truth, and that the ordinary mind is not reliable. But surely all our knowledge of life and of ourselves is based on a reliable understanding of facts. Surely Sufis are only talking about a minority of people. If they are, why bother with them?

A: On the contrary, Sufis are talking here about a majority of people. It is interesting to note that it is only lately that others are catching up with this very great problem. I call it a problem because if it is true that people ordinarily are prone to considerable mistakes in perception and understanding, and are easily misled by wrong information, then this stands, as the Sufis say, as a barrier to real understanding.

This has been demonstrated again and again. On television, in one programme as an example, it was shown that people hardly ever know what they have seen: 'as eye-witnesses, humans are in the disaster class'.*

From 525 questions asked of witnesses to staged events, only 52 – one in ten – were correct: and this from a selection of people who had been alerted to watch for something and still could not see it. The social consequences might include people being imprisoned on inaccurate eye-witness testimony. The consequences for the perception of things which are there in a higher sense are what the Sufis talk about.

This opens the question of who can learn, and what is a student.

*Daily Telegraph, London: February 21 1974, p. 12 ('Evidence of your Eyes' programme).

116

Again, people ask for truth, but advertisers have sh
truth does not sell goods. A study presented before the
Marketing Association showed that truthful advertiser
but lying ones succeed, in putting people into a buying

In supposedly religious matters which have been shown to be
early examples of 'advertising', the same picture emerges. The
Glastonbury legends, in which, among other things, Christ
himself appeared and dedicated a church, are only one example.
Supposed to start from AD 63, the scheme was in reality started as
a fund-raising ploy in 1184 – 1,121 years after the supposed
events, by the monks, whose buildings had been destroyed by a
fire. Does anyone believe that supposed events of over a thousand
years ago, first published today as true fact, should receive any
credence?†

This human tendency has actually been tested. The BBC 2 television man Tony Bilbow hoaxed viewers by saying that he had
obtained film clips of 'The Great Pismo' and showed forgeries of
the film. Then:

'Everybody began to remember The Great Pismo when he made
his television debut. Letters piled into the BBC praising the
1920's comedian.

'A woman wrote enthusiastically: "My aunt was a great fan of
the Great Pismo – she saw him at a show in Hastings." She added:
"What a pity he was not recognized on television before she died in
1957." One man even sent in photographs of The Great Pismo's
father.' (*Daily Sketch*, June 26, 1969, page 9.)

After all that, could one doubt that he ever existed?

It is precisely because of the unreliability of vision, of memory,
of wanting to believe, of induced belief: whether in religion, in
motor accidents, or in the lives of invented individuals, that the
Sufis say that an objective perception must be acquired before
even familiar things can be seen as they are.

What do you Really Know?

*Q: The sensitivity of people towards animals must surely help
them to understand higher things, especially the ability of animal-*

Time Magazine, New York: May 14, 1973, p. 62 ('Truth Doesn't Sell').
†*The Times*, London: May 28, 1976, quoting *Christianity in Somerset,* edited by Dr.
Robert Dunning, London 1976 (Somerset County Council).

117

lovers to perceive directly the ways of their pets?

A: That is quite true; however, before you attribute this ability to all animal-lovers, consider what a number of cat-fanciers thought about cats. They were asked:

1. Are cats lone animals?
2. Do they form gangs, especially the males?
3. Do dominant males challenge others for the favours of the females?
4. Do they invariably react against intrusion of other cats into their territory?
5. Do dominant cats try to drive weaker ones from the latter's territory?
6. Are some domestic cats unable to kill?

Out of these six questions, asked from a hundred cat-fanciers, each person got every answer wrong.

The answers, by the way, are: questions 1, 3, 4, and 5, NO; questions 2 and 6, YES.

This research, by Professor Paul Leyhauser of the West German Max Planck Institute, showed that people may think that they know about animals, but do they?

Similarly, what people think that they know (even thinking that they know it by observation and even experience) about other things, such as psychological and religious matters, can often be seen to be fragmentary, misplaced, selectively adopted.

If people could rely upon themselves to learn by themselves, they would not need teaching. They wouldn't even need scientific verifications of fact to correct them, because their beliefs would be based on accurate information, since they would either observe correctly from the beginning or else reject inaccurate information.

So, before we get to the point of the value of the knowledge, we must be sure that it is really there.

Human Nature

Q: *The Sufis often condemn heedlessness, irrelevance and confusion, and insist that these things have to be set aside since they interfere with higher perceptions, keeping people 'asleep' for practical purposes. But are those characteristics manifested in ordinary*

*life, and if they are how do they affect us? If so, is this an analogy of
the barriers to higher understanding?*

A: I should have thought that any of these factors would interfere with the effectiveness of almost anything in ordinary life. But
that they are part of ordinary human behaviour has been tested. A
recent example is the nature of inventors and the characteristics
of those whom they have to deal with in the matter of inventions.

When the journal *New Scientist* carried out an investigation
into the question, it was able to publish results* which showed
that this is a general human problem. The inventors were frequently irrelevant, confused and impatient. Some tried to patent
inventions that nobody wanted because they were doing something which was already done. Some let their patents lapse. They
wrote letters which could hardly be read, which dealt with
divorce, illness, burglary and surgery as well as the invention supposedly under discussion. Sometimes when asked about one
invention they would answer about another. They changed their
addresses without informing the Patents Office, so they could not
be contacted.

The reaction to inventions was just as bad, or worse. Major
official and other entities completely misunderstood inventions
although they were supposed to be evaluating them. Some organisations did not like them when they had not been carried out by
their own staff. Some people liked inventions but did not believe
that they would work, though they could not say why. Some of the
reasons why inventions were turned down were obviously absurd.
One invention which saves lives after cardiac arrest, for instance,
was disliked because the release of an air valve made a hissing
sound! The Minister at the Department of Health completely misunderstood one remarkable invention to prevent suicide or
accidental death through introducing emetics into tablets. People
felt that their empire would be threatened by the acceptance of an
outside invention. The Press preferred lamenting the increase in
car thefts to featuring an invention to frustrate them. And, in the
case of the same invention, everyone approached thought it so
simple that it could not work.

Here we have the classic working of the major human, normal
methods of thinking and acting – or not acting:

Laziness, stupidity, incredulity, fear of upsetting the *status quo*,
obstructionism, timidity, irrelevance and confusion and so on.

It should be remembered that when the ordinary human being
is approached with an idea, a series of ideas, or a teaching, he or
she will often respond in just this same way. It is because of this

*Adrian Hope: 'It's a wonderful idea, but . . .', in *New Scientist*, 1 June 1978, pp. 576
ff.

119

that people with new things to say have resorted to arousing the greed of whomever they are approaching. This succeeds in increasing the greed and preventing the development of any side of the character or of the proposal which is not connected with greed.

There is not only an analogy with higher understanding here. Before we get to that, we have to deal with the barriers erected by the 'lower understanding,' which often cannot be described as understanding at all.

The Sufi perception of these problems has been continually and solidly represented for centuries. The Sufi activity is designed to get past these barriers, by the methods indicated to out-manoeuvre the 'Commanding Self', which is the complex of reactions involved when presenting advanced ideas to ordinary people and organisations.

This experience with an easily-studied area of human activity startlingly illustrates how 'humanity is asleep'.

New Knowledge from Old

Q: By what method do the Sufis extract information of value to present-day psychology and higher knowledge from ancient written materials? For my own part, I can only see the ordinary meaning in such texts.

A: This is an interesting question, and the only way to answer it is to say that one has to have specialised knowledge and also experience. But it may be possible to make the process clearer by means of an analogy.

Assume that there is a water source which seems unexpectedly to be harming crops. An expert is called in and he realises that there is zeolite in the water and that it is no longer active. He also knows that salt can regenerate it, by means of the following formula:

$$CaZe + 2\,NaCl = Na_2Ze + CaCl_2.$$

He adds salt to the water and the phenomenon of ion exchange is achieved.

So we need a chemist.

Now, if you are still with me, consider the following passage from the Old Testament (II Kings 2, 19–21):

> And the men of the city said unto Elisha, Behold, I pray thee, the situation of this city is pleasant, and as my Lord seeth: but the water is naught, and the ground barren. And he said, Bring me a new cruse, and put salt therein. And they brought it to him. And he went forth unto the spring of the waters, and cast the salt in there, and said, Thus saith the Lord, I have healed these waters; there shall not be from thence any more death or barren land.

It is difficult to imagine that Elisha is not demonstrating chemical knowledge and performing ion exchange.

If you did not know something about chemistry, the story might make an interesting read about a miracle. On the other hand, if you did, it makes, for some at least, an even more interesting account of information.

You may be interested to know that the chemical nature of this Biblical tale, reaching beyond its supposed miracle status, was analysed by Professor Yahia Haschmi, an illustrious scientist and Sufi authority of the Aleppo Society for Scientific Research, in Syria in 1962*

Floor Covering

Q: I was interested to read in the Press that you are reported as having said that institutions, far from giving a guarantee of rationality because they are subject to assessment and measurement, equally often, or more frequently, enshrine irrationality. But surely, whereas a quasi-institution like a commercial company may behave eccentrically because of the wishes of, say, the Directors, this is not the case in more coherent bodies like Government Departments, where there is a public check?

A: The tendency is everywhere. Rather than my wasting your time with numerous examples, I think that it would be worth your while to seek such anomalies yourself. There are to be found in the newspapers, if you have no direct contacts to supply them. Here is just one:

The *New Scientist* reported on 29 March 1979 that the following

*M. Y. Haschmi: 'Ion Exchange in Arabic Alchemy', in *Ithaca*, 26 VIII – 2 IX 1962.

figures had been given in the British Parliament for the underfoot floor covering supplied by the Government for various kinds of people in its employ:

Typists: £25
Clerical officers £30
Senior executive officers: £67
Undersecretaries: £181
Deputy secretary: £290.

There is no evidence that Deputy Secretaries' office floors get harder treatment than Undersecretaries'; indeed, there is nothing to show that such carpets *are* harder-wearing – only that they are more expensive. We all know, of course, that a better carpet is a hallowed privilege, and that people are reprimanded for using their own rugs if these seem to indicate a higher status. But where does the rug as an indicator of status connect with the rationality expected from an institution?

Economics

Q: Although, as we know, most Sufi activity down the ages has been private rather than public, and Sufis do not primarily wish to attract attention to themselves, there is undoubtedly evidence of a massive investment of people and resources in Sufi teaching. Apart from the scholars, who are subsidised by universities, and the cultists, who are self-financing as they grow in numbers, there are the Sufi activities which appear full-blown, and which are always seen to be immensely efficient and well funded. What makes it worth while for the Sufis to engage in such enormous investments?

A: Sufi activity is, of course, to be expressed more in terms of less impressive-looking things than material investment. But, as you have raised the matter, you might care to look at it in this way, by pursuing your own line of thought:

We can take the smallpox eradication programme of the United Nations as an equivalence. This started in 1968 and lasted for a decade. The United States alone contributed $2.6 million a year towards the effort – $26 million over the ten years in which the disease was eliminated.

Now, many people imagined that this money was lost, was of

122

the nature of charity to the Third World; and some wondered whether it could not be better used in the U.S.A. itself. 'Why do we spend such massive sums on people who often don't behave properly?' it was asked.

Dr. L. B. Brilliant of the World Health Organisation's Smallpox Eradication Programme, however, has revealed that the United States of America *alone* gains over $300 million each year in savings on her protection of the American people against smallpox. Others calculate the saving as being in excess of 450 million dollars, again annually.

So your word 'investment' is correct. Sufis invest partly to protect the people against the absence of Sufic activity and consequent impoverishment of the people, and partly in order to 'inoculate' the people against cults and conditioning; and partly to bring the advantages of the Sufi enterprise to the people who can benefit from them.

Similarly, too, people who contribute to Sufi entities also help to prevent things getting worse; and they also help to make it impossible for things ever to be as bad again as they once were.

Invention versus Development

Q: British people constantly complain that, although they invent some of the most wonderful things, they hardly ever develop them, and the result is that technical devices all over the world are of British origin, while engineers and scientists of other nations adapt and market them. What can be done about this, and what is its relevance to higher human capacities?

A: I have heard this constantly: about antibiotics, about jet engines, about hovercraft, and so on. People love to complain about it in speeches, and it is part of a refrain seen in the newspapers. The implication is that, if one could only develop a better planning and vision sense, all would be well.

Before looking at this problem, I think that it is worth paying attention to what an Englishman said, after considering the whole phenomenon. He told me:

'A Frenchman, a German and an Englishman were being taken to be hanged. The Frenchman was first, and the trapdoor did not work. He was reprieved on the grounds that nobody could be hanged twice: fate had intervened. The same thing happened to the German.

'As the Englishman was being taken for his turn, he was asked if he had any last words."Yes",he said,"you need a bit of grease on the hinges!"'

The joke itself is remarkably diagnostic of the mentality in question. The man knows what should be done, but is unable to relate it to his own needs. He is unable, too, to keep his mouth shut, even when his life is at stake.

This, in turn, highlights the problem. If human beings are dependent upon invention and the development of inventions without any question as to what kinds of inventions, when and where, would be of any far-reaching value, then those who invent will have to learn how to develop, and those who develop should also learn to invent, if this kind of thing is to be kept going satisfactorily to such a mechanistic view of life.

But what about the matter of what kind of inventions and what kind of development? For this, higher knowledge is necessary.

Deterrent

Q: I can't understand how it can be true that real Sufi teachings contain elements which deter unsuitable people from going deeper into the subject, on a deliberate basis. Surely the intention of the Sufis, like that of everyone having something good to share, is to interest as many people as possible, and to improve people by means of their literature, not to deflect them?

A: People are always writing to other people, claiming that they 'can't understand' this or that. Now, if they do not understand it, this is merely a statement of the reader's condition – it is not a question. If, on the other hand, the individual means that he does not want to believe it, we might try to give an answer. I choose to interpret this question in that way.

On the social level, people often make themselves obnoxious to others to prevent them from trying to become too friendly, if they do not like them. Do you imagine that something which can operate on such a crude level cannot be worked on a higher one? Rumi, for instance, constantly assails scholars and shows them up as much more stupid than they imagine themselves to be. This deters few scholars: they continue to write and lecture about Rumi and his work. But it gives the ordinary person an opportunity to see the absurdity of the situation: scholars repeating their own shortcomings, and continuing to do Rumi's work after seven hundred years.

In assuming that the Sufis want to share and interest as many people as possible, you are confusing them with enthusiast cultists and people who count heads. The Sufis want to share, but they have to share with those who can profit from the sharing and can therefore continue the process of sharing with others to come. This requires the Sufis using their energy in 'teaching how to learn', before any sharing can take place. Sharing the sheer sensation of importance or of being a human being or even a servant of humanity, can be done by anyone, and is the sort of sharing that people are always straining towards. But the minimum human duty is to serve others: it is no great attainment. Feeling important is a vice, not a virtue, however concealed as participation in something noble.

Finally, note what New Jersey park officials in the U.S.A. have done with Christmas trees. So many people were stealing them that they are now sprayed with a chemical which gives off an offensive smell when the tree is put in a warm place.* Thieves learn to avoid these trees for this reason. If this can be done with plants, why not with books? And, in the case of a book, or a man's behaviour, even, you don't have to ruin the book or waste the man's contact (as you have to ruin the Christmas trees of New Jersey) to teach the 'can't-understanders' a lesson.

Cause and Effect

Q: Why do Sufis sometimes do inexplicable things? I have heard of them forbidding people to eat certain food, or telling them to go to certain places, or even saying outrageous things which people puzzle over for years.

A: Imitators do these things to impress. Real Sufis do them because they have a knowledge of cause and effect. Most people have no idea that the most trivial-seeming actions may have extremely far-reaching effects. Only occasionally are cause and

Daily Telegraph, London: 19 December 1978, p. 8, Cols. 4–5.

effect seen in a short run within a contracted time-scale, giving an equivalence of what we are talking about. There is the case, to take one almost at random, of

THE WINE AND THE FINGER

The French playwright Victorien Sardou was sitting at table during a dinner when he upset a glass of wine. A lady by his side, to prevent the liquid staining the cloth, poured salt on it. Spilt salt, to some people, means bad luck. To counteract this, a pinch is thrown over the shoulder; and Sardou did just this.

The salt got into the eyes of the waiter who was trying to serve him, and the chicken on a plate which he held fell to the ground. The dog of the house started to gobble the chicken, and a bone lodged in its throat so that it began to choke. The hostess's son tried to get the bone out of the dog's throat. Now the dog turned on the youth and bit his finger so hard that it had to be amputated.

The waiter, the dog and the son of the house were all acting automatically, through the secondary self: a mixture of greed, hope, fear and conditioning. Only the woman acted for practical reasons: but her attempt to retrieve the situation was foiled by the playwright, whose second action – throwing the salt over his shoulder – set the whole train of actions going.

False Masters

Q: Why are there so many false spiritual teachers around?
A: This is one of the most common questions, and there are almost as many answers as there are people asking. When there is a true or useful thing, there is sure to be a counterfeit. This does not mean that the original intention was bad: but things turn out bad if they are not properly organised. There is no difference between this problem and the one of the

LOVELORN TAIWANESE

There was once a young man of Taiwan who desperately desired that a certain girl should marry him. He wrote her letters, over a period of two years, an average of one a day, declaring his love.

126

This continued, says the United Press, from 1972 to 1976.

Without that effort it is unlikely that the lady would have become engaged, in the way she did, to the postman who delivered the letters.

Troubadours

Q: I have heard it said, repeatedly, that such groupings as the Troubadours were engaged in religious enlightenment programmes; but I cannot see how. After all, they were amusing people with their songs and poems. Surely this is part of what you have called the 'entertainment industry', and would not bring anyone to enlightenment, any more than sacred dances or self-centred prayer?

A: There is a restaurant in New York to which a kind friend took me. The waiters there entertain the children with balloons and songs and doing a pied-piper act around the tables. Does this make anyone imagine that they are not waiters at all? A moment's observation shows that, in addition to this entertainment function, they are indeed workers, bringing food to the tables.

The fact is that Sufi activities may contain entertainment value, but they have something else as well; just as an orange has flavour and nutrition. This is not widely understood only because people are in fact looking for entertainment, or else to denigrate it, they are not looking for fact. Here is a tale which may fix this in your mind:

A man used to stand outside the window of a beautiful girl, playing the guitar and serenading her.

Someone asked:

'Why do you not ask her to marry you?'

He said:

'I have thought of that; but, if she agreed, what would I do with my evenings?'

127

7
REMARKS AT THE
DINNER-MEETINGS

Satisfaction

Q: Why is it that so many people are satisfied with vain and stupid things? Surely it is obvious that there are objectives higher than making money, or playing games, or trying for fame, for instance?

A: People can only do what they can do at any given moment. They may have to wait until circumstances allow them to have better aims.

There is a story about this, which may have a parallel in the familiar world:

THE REMEDY

An insomniac went to a devout doctor for advice.

'Memorize prayers, and sit up all night repeating them' said the holy physician.

'And will that cure my sleeplessness?'

'No, but it will cease to annoy you.'

Bases and Essentials of Sufi Knowledge

A man once noticed a very large, locked box, which seemed very old and was of curious workmanship, in the corner of the shop of one of the great merchants of Baghdad.

On the outside was inscribed:

The Bases and Essentials of Sufi Knowledge

Now this man was interested, for he had been reflecting about the Sufis for many years, and reading their works and about their lives.

131

He bought the box for a very large sum of money, and took it home.

When he managed to open it, there was only a small piece of paper inside, on which was written: 'The Bases and Essentials of Sufi knowledge are that you desire truth above excitement and that you make your way to the Teacher.'

Who is the More Spiritual?

Q: How is it that higher ideas and deeper insights always come from the East?

A: I can give you one of the explanations which are current in the East. It was known there at least as long ago as the Crusades, but I think that you will find it contains an interesting hidden reflection about human nature:

It is related that a young man asked a sage:

'How is it that the Franks have so much brute force, while we only have faith?'

'Because', said the wise man, 'when provisions for this world were being handed out at the beginning – they had the first choice.'

Recognising It

A group of people all died at once in a catastrophe, and were surprised to find themselves in a world very much like this one. All kinds of entertainments and every possible facility were provided.

They were amazed to learn that they were in Hell.

Those who wanted exciting lives got them. People who desired money received it. Ambitions of all kinds were fulfilled.

There were many demons in attendance, who helped everyone to do what they wanted.

One day, known as 'complaints day', a number of the inmates went to the controlling demon and said:

'We have a wonderful life: parties, riches, excitement. But we seem to be withering away, become unattractive to each other little by little, lose the belongings that come to us so easily....'

'Yes', said the fiend, 'Hell, isn't it?'

The King and his Son

Once there was a king, whose only son chose, as he grew up, to be an idler and spendthrift. Constantly surrounded by wasters and opportunists – whom he regarded as really worthwhile people – he judged everything by their standards. Although all lived, for example, through the bounty of the King, they mocked him in private and thought highly of people and things which were of no value at all, apart from amusing them.

One day the King, without warning, called the Prince and had him thrown out of the palace. Unhappy and bewildered, the youth went from one of his friends to the next, seeking sympathy and comfort, asking for help. But none would aid him – apart from saying that the King must be an evil man, and there surely was justice somewhere, probably as far from the Palace as could be.

Because of his foolishness and habits, the Prince felt more and more estranged from his father. Although he tried to make a new life for himself, he did not know how to do so. He had forgotten, in the company of his evil associates who posed as friends, how to see things as they really are. Consequently he found his life both hard and perplexing. He engaged himself in trivial pursuits, haunted all the same by anxiety and emptiness.

After many months, the King sent emissaries to bring the Prince before him. 'My son,' he said, 'you surely see how your own habits have laid you low, and how little use to you your formerly valued companions have been.'

We, too, who rely upon certain aims in this life as 'good' and esteem certain things and people as 'significant', must fail to see the Real, or even its indications. Certain habits of mind hold us fast, in the role of 'idlers' and 'spendthrifts.'

Definitions

A good man is one who treats others as he would like to be treated.

A generous man is one who treats others better than he expects to be treated.

A wise man is one who knows how he and others should be treated: in what ways, and to what extent.

The first man is a civilising influence.

The second man is a refining and spreading influence.

The third man is a higher-development influence.

Everyone should go through the three phases typified by these three men.

To believe that goodness or generosity are ends in themselves may be good or it may be generous. It is, however, not an informed attitude – and that is the most good and the most generous we can be about it.

If someone said: 'Is it better to be good, generous or wise?' one would have to reply:

'If you are wise, you do not have to be obsessed by being "good" or "generous". You are obliged to do what is necessary.'

The Guru

The East teems with people who are seeking knowledge and have come from the West with no background to enable them to recognise it.

And it is seething, too, with tales about these people and their peculiar ways. When you meet them back in Europe or America and they tell you how they found truth, take it with a pinch of salt.

One of my favourite stories of these unfortunates is this one:

ONLY A MATTER OF TIME

A Western seeker-after-Truth went on a journey to the East, with a number of photographs which a friend had given him of a supposed spiritual teacher. To make it easier, the friend had sent him eight pictures of the same man, taken from different angles.

After some weeks, such is the multitude of alleged mystics in those parts, he got a postcard from his friend, which said:

'I have located and been spiritually elevated by seven of the great men whose photographs you sent me, and I am hot on the trail of the eighth!'

Critiques of Sufism

All current critiques of Sufism can be assessed when it is realised that analysis, discussion and investigation of opposing arguments show them to be based on one or more of these few simple factors:

1. A desire to maintain intact in his mind ideas or assumptions which the critic fears Sufi thought threatens;

2. A desire to find in Sufism an over-simplified system, failing which the critic may well oppose the form with which he is in contact, or else oppose all of Sufism. This is due to failing in the search for a mental model of Sufism which the critic may accept, one which accords with his prejudices, however formed.

3. Lack of information and relatively shallow study. Sufi thought and action being so widespread in various languages, cultures and times, scholars and students often mistake a local manifestation for 'all of Sufism', or 'the real Sufism'. A variety of this is found in personality worship, when loyalty to an individual Sufi teacher causes his followers to regard emphases which he has made as sacrosanct, and those which he has not made as heterodox. This is only a normal development in cult-formation and is, of course, taking the student out of Sufism into factionism.

It is interesting, if not remarkable, to note that whereas Sufism is systematised only for instrumental purposes – to approach objectives – and cannot therefore be approached through simplistic means, yet the critical approaches to it are so intensely over-simplified as to be virtually covered by the three main factors listed above.

Innumerable books, reviews, letters and lectures which have been analysed during the past decade or so show an overwhelming ascendancy of reactions to Sufism which fall within these categories.

Side-Effects

Q: Since I began to study Sufism, there have been many difficulties in my life; or it may be that I notice things more than I did. I often feel that the disadvantages are greater than the benefits.

A: This is a typical question, and one of the interesting things about it is that an equal number of people say the very reverse. Both comments, of course, emanate from the shallower part of the mind, and have to do with expectation.

This part of one's mind is very well represented by various animals in fables and other literature. The situation of this questioner can be summed up in the saying:

'A donkey drank from a pool and then complained that his chin became wet.'

According to the Best Advice

Q: There is a widespread tendency today for people to amalgamate beliefs and rituals from all spiritual sources. Sufis, however, seem to say that truth is one and forms vary and cannot be amalgamated. If all forms are only part of an ultimate truth, why cannot these forms be associated together?

A: Because the forms date from various needs and epochs, and do not go together, any more than the wheel of a horse-carriage will fit a motor-car.

Perhaps you have not heard the tale of Mulla Nasrudin, when he was trying to build a house?

His friends, all of whom had houses and some of whom were carpenters, builders and so on, surrounded him. He was glad to have their advice.

One after the other, and sometimes all together, they told him what to do. Mulla Nasrudin obediently followed the instructions of each one.

136

When the building was finished, it looked nothing like a house. 'That's funny,' said Nasrudin, 'after all, I did do exactly what everyone told me to!'

Sweets for the Wise

There is a very ancient tale about two scholars, much respected in their communities, who were out for a walk one day, discussing people and affairs, when the conversation turned to the subject of a certain prominent Sufi.

The first man of learning, whose favourite subject was literature and biography, said of the Sufi:

'He is a true sage, and a saint; he never takes anything for himself.'

The second savant, whose expertise was in religion and who had much experience of legal affairs, said:

'He does not have to "take" – for people automatically give things to him. I am sure, however, that he would take if he could...'

Thus engaged, each offering in turn an anecdote about the Sufi to support his own contentions, the two reflective ones came upon a caravanserai. They entered it, attracted by the sound of a loud and animated discussion. Inside they found a woman, repeating to a circle of merchants, idlers and others:

'I have been divorced by my husband, and I have lost my marriage contract, by the terms of which I am entitled to half of his possessions if he divorces me. Now he denies having signed it; and the Court will not listen to me. I have only a single copper coin to my name.' The audience were offering suggestions to solve her problem, ranging from murder to prayer.

The second scholar now suggested that the matter should be taken to the Sufi whom they had been discussing, for his intervention. 'In this way' he said to his companion, 'we can establish whether he will in fact do anything for nothing.'

Now, since the Sufi was so highly respected, everyone agreed, and all present at once went to the place where this man of wisdom sat, silently, for an hour before dinner on one day a week.

The crowd ranged themselves around the contemplating sage, who raised his eyes to the distraught woman. 'What do you want?'

137

he asked, and she said:

'Respected Sir, these two wise and kindly gentlemen have suggested that you might help me. Would you come to the magistrates to testify that, from your looking into my heart, I am telling the truth when I say that by my lost marriage contract I am entitled to half of my former husband's goods upon being divorced? The Court will judge only on evidence, or upon the word of one who is related to the truth...'

The Sufi interrupted her. 'Before we do anything like that, you will have to do something else. Go to the market and bring me a piece of Turkish delight.'

Now the crowd gasped, the first scholar felt acutely embarrassed at the Sufi's greed and superficiality, and the second scholar smiled in triumph at this apparent demonstration of the mystic's true nature. The woman, after a moment's thought, scowled, turned on her heel and went off to buy the sweetmeat.

Everyone waited in silence, until the woman returned and threw a packet, bought with her last coin, at the Sufi's feet. 'Is this the way to behave when you seek a favour?' asked the Sufi; 'pray open the packet and remove the confection.'

As the woman unwrapped the package, she saw that it was enfolded in a piece of paper, the very same one upon which was written her marriage contract.

Now, of course, the crowd howled with delight at the miracle; the first scholar was filled with joy, and the second man of learning felt abashed and confused.

When the members of the crowd had run off in all directions to spread word of the miracle of the great saint, and the woman and the two men of words still stood before him, the Sufi said, to the woman:

'Know that your needs can often be fulfilled, but that the way to achieve this is seldom by giving specific instructions to those who know better. Now go and get your rights.'

To the first scholar he said:

'To judge a person as "good" through judgment based on superficialities is only slightly better than to judge him "bad" by outward signs. Try to learn what really is right, not to follow what happens to please you.'

To the second scholar he said:

'For the bitterness of disappointment in what is really a shallow way of thinking, the remedy is to take something as paltry but more sweet. I therefore award you the Turkish delight – trivial to deal with trivial. As for the onlookers – they have had their sustenance, for they sought excitement.'

And, although this happened many centuries ago, it is insisted by the Wise that similar events can be seen by those who will see them, being played out in the world of today, and every day.

✓ Alarm

Q: The dangers of personality-worship and the need for everyone to find his own way are the most attractive statements of a certain guru, who has many disciples all over the world. Should he not be listened to?

A: There is a saying:

'Do not fell a tree which is giving shade.' Many people imagine that such gurus as this are holy and useful. They are, in fact, providing a distinguished social (though not a spiritual) service. Those who need this 'shade' should certainly have it.

As for others, they should be able to know what is shade and what is something else.

The way to determine this is to look and see whether, in the words of another proverb, some people are 'Feeding a flame and crying "Fire"!'

✓ A Basic Pattern

If you collect a number of the most frequent reasons said to be given by women to explain why they want something, you might be rather surprised when comparing them with supposedly 'less frivolous' desires. On the left is a list of the 'reasons' or justifications advanced by women; on the right, taken from my own files, actual examples of reasons given to me why various correspondents think they should study to be Sufis:

1 It is good for my morale	1 I want to be happy/fulfilled
2 It is from Paris	2 It is from the East
3 Everybody has one	3 Everyone is entitled to knowledge
4 Nobody else has one	4 It is rare knowledge/for the few
5 It is cheaper in the long run	5 It may be harder, but it is more real

139

6 It is different	6 It is different
7 I have waited so long	7 I have waited all my life
8 I like it: it must be right	8 Something tells me it must be true
9 I have always wanted one...	9 The need has always been in me

There is no doubt that both the wanting of the adornment and of the more subtle 'spiritual' satisfaction are varieties of an acquisition impulse in these cases.

Sufis are aware that this stage must be passed. To get beyond this acquisition point it may be necessary to reach it first, recognise it and then discard it.

There are three useful reflections which apply to the description and superseding of this state:

1. If I worship You for desire for Paradise, exclude me from Paradise; if I worship You for fear of Hell, cast me into Hell (Rabia).

2. The donkey which brought you to the door is not the means by which you enter the house.

3. First repent: afterwards you have to repent your repentance.

✓ Impact

It is characteristic of the primitive to regard things which are felt strongly to be of great importance. The less the person knows about the origin or working of the feeling, the greater importance he is likely to endow it with. Take a few almost random examples:

* Unable to explain or to mitigate the pains of childbirth, primitive people have come to regard them as inflicted by some higher power. Some people believe this even today. The 'sophisticated barbarian' takes this thinking a stage further, and actually believes that the mother's love for her child is in direct proportion to the pain which she experienced during its delivery. This tells you nothing about mother-love, but everything about those who believe this.

* If a primitive person, or a child at a similar stage of mental development, experiences a pain, or a sense of joy, in accidental synchronicity with some other event, he or she will often link the two, producing a sense of importance for what might well have been a trivial or irrelevant event.

* If you follow up the history of an individual who regards some personality as being of great importance in his life, you will always find that the personality has at some time engendered strong feelings of some sort in the other person.

 • The fact is that emotion sensitises the brain of the individual. If no true explanation of what is happening (such as 'you are only having a tooth out') is forthcoming, a strong sense of dependency towards the source (or even a supposed source) of the stimulus will take its place. Instead of explanation the brain will resort to quasi-explanation.

 • Such a quasi-explanation may become so powerful that it can assume a dominant position in the mental picture of the individual.

 • It is the conscious or unconscious policy of many religious, political, social, tribal, psychological, scholastic and other dogmatic bodies to create this situation in the expectation that at the moment of greatest emotion the commanding idea which is to take possession of the individual's mind will be the one which the system itself desires to propagate.

 This pattern may be seen repeated somewhere in virtually every system in the world. It also occurs, repeatedly, randomly and accidentally. When a person acquires a fixation upon some bizarre and unacceptable idea, the condition attracts the attention of psychological therapists. When it is 'harmless', it may not be perceived at all. When it is socially acceptable, the individual may even be rewarded, and the conditioning reinforced by each reward.

 • In practical philosophies we again and again find that the basic attempt (before the institutional or dogmatic phase) must be to enable the learner to see himself as the victim of such forces. By detachment from the operation of impact upon himself, he is able, theoretically, to prevent the operation of emotion in making him not himself, but a copy of someone else or the product of a series of ideas.

 • Until this stage of understanding is reached, indeed, all efforts to understand oneself, to find who one really is, are at best of latent value; because they will always be evaluated through the veil of the very obsessions implanted by the mechanisms just described.

8
THE SKILL THAT
NOBODY HAS:
Twelve Tales

The Skill that Nobody Has

There was, in far-off times, a youth who lived near a small town in a mighty empire. He was bright and intelligent, and he impressed everyone with his ability to learn and his good-neighbourliness.

He lived with his widowed mother.

One day his mother said to him, 'Anwar' – for that was his name, 'Anwar, you should really be thinking about settling down in life. True, you help the farmers like other lads. I know that you sit at home and make baskets like other people, when there is nothing else to do. But you should either get married or set forth to seek your fortune in the wider world. At any rate, that is what I think about things.'

'My dear Mother!' cried the boy, 'that is exactly what I want to do. I could stay at home and work permanently for one of the farmers; or I could go and try something really reckless, like travelling to very distant parts. But, before attempting anything like that, I have made up my mind that I shall both stay fairly near to home and also become someone of importance: I shall marry the daughter of the Emperor and live happily ever after!'

'People like us', said the old lady, 'do not usually have such ideas. Why, hardly any of us ordinary working folk has ever seen the Emperor, much less his daughter. And who are you, may I ask, to go to our monarch and ask such an outrageous thing?'

'I, Mother, am nobody to do so,' said the youth; 'but *you*, now – that is another matter. I want you to go to the Emperor and ask for the Princess for a daughter-in-law!'

We can well imagine how the poor old thing felt. The boy Anwar was, it is true, the apple of her eye, but surely he was showing far too much recklessness and even rudeness in having such ambitions?

'Nonsense!' she said, and set him to do so much work that for a time he forgot his plan.

Then something reminded him again. He badgered his mother until she gave up, packed a bag with a few essentials, and made

145

her way to the capital of the Empire.

Day after day the poor woman loitered near the palace, where she saw the glittering guard ride forth, the embassies from far-off lands arrive and depart, the towering walls behind which sat, in his throne-room, the Emperor himself. There was plenty of excitement in the streets, as there always is in a capital city. Processions and people of importance were everywhere, and both of them, in their own proper place, were for the edification of the people.

But how does one actually get into the presence of such a person as an emperor?

She tried and tried and tried. Then she thought, 'If the Emperor won't let me go to him, I must wait until he comes to me!'

So she stationed herself, day and night, outside the great mosque to which the Emperor rode, on a white horse, to pray on Fridays. There was always a large crowd there, but after a time the old woman became known as the one who sat at a certain point. She chose this spot because it was just where the ruler turned his horse after mounting it.

One Friday, then, she was sitting quietly in her usual position, when, as the Emperor put his foot into the stirrup and glanced in her direction, she raised her hands in supplication.

'Have that woman brought to the Palace', ordered the monarch as soon as he saw her gesture. In a few minutes she was beside him in the throne-room.

'You are a poor woman, as I can see,' said His Majesty, 'and you had better speak if you seek a boon from me!'

But the woman was so awestruck by the place, and by being actually talking to the great man, that, although she opened her mouth, no sound came forth from it.

So the Emperor ordered that she be given a bag of gold and shown the door, 'These people can always do with money', he said to his courtiers.

When the old lady returned home, her son said, 'Did you see the Emperor?'

'Indeed, I did, Anwar!'

'Did you appeal to him?'

'I did.'

'Did you enter his presence?'

'Yes.'

'And what did he say to my proposal of marriage to his daughter, the Princess Salma?'

'Foolish boy! How could I, dressed in rags and without any of the manners of the court, say a thing like that? I said nothing, for I was overcome with the splendour of the place. But His Imperial

146

Majesty was more than kind, and has given us this bag, heavy with gold. You can use it to set yourself up in trade, and that will give you a career and a lifetime's fulfilment. Forget all this nonsense about princesses!'

'Mother, I don't want gold, I want the Princess!' said Anwar.

He continued to pester her, until she was forced to set off, once again, to the capital.

There the Emperor saw her again, sitting in her corner. He called her to him and again asked her what she wanted. Again she was too frightened to speak. Again he gave her a bag of gold and sent her away.

And the same thing happened when she returned to her humble cottage, with Anwar not at all reconciled, after all the Emperor's kindness.

Finally, Anwar said to his mother, 'I have decided not to stay at home. I have decided not to accept the comfortable life which the gold would give me. I have decided to seek the Emperor's daughter, and I shall therefore set off tomorrow morning to find out how I can win her.'

The next day, as dawn broke, he left the house and started to walk along the road, through the woods. As the road turned at the top of a hill, Anwar came across a wise man, sitting by the way, with a pointed cap on his head, his robe made up of small squares of rag carefully stitched together.

'Peace upon you, Your Presence the Dervish!' said Anwar politely.

'And what do you seek, little brother?' asked the dervish.

'I am seeking the way in which I can approach the Emperor and ask for the hand of his daughter in marriage, for I have set my heart upon it,' said Anwar.

'That is difficult' said the wise man, 'unless you are first prepared to learn the "Skill that Nobody Has".'

'How can there be such a thing, if it is called the "Skill that *Nobody* Has"?' asked the youth.

'Nobody has it because people *do* it,' said the dervish, 'and they can only *do* it when they *have* something, some other things. When they have the things, the skill works for them, so they don't really have to have it.'

'This is extremely difficult' said Anwar, 'but can you tell me how to go about it?'

'Yes, indeed,' said the old man. 'You keep straight on, allowing nothing to deflect you, sticking with the same road, and not thinking that anything is more important than the road.'

Anwar thanked the dervish and went on his way. The road led him on and on, and he lived as best he could on wild fruits, roots and berries and the kindness of various people whom he met. From time to time people suggested that he should take up employment with them, or interest himself in their crafts and occupations; or even marry their daughters. But Anwar kept on, although after a very long time he began to feel, more and more, that the road was leading nowhere at all.

And then, one day, as it was coming to nightfall, Anwar saw that the road did indeed end. That is to say, instead of passing a certain towering fortress, it led straight within the walls, through a wide gate.

Anwar followed it in.

The gatekeeper challenged him:

'What do you seek?'

'I am in search of the Princess, whom I am determined to marry', answered Anwar.

'You cannot pass, unless you have a more reasonable object than that!' shouted the guardian of the gate, and he levelled a sharpened spike at poor Anwar.

Anwar said: 'Well, then, I am going to learn the "Skill that Nobody Has"'.

'That's different,' said the guard, lowering his weapon; 'but,' he added sulkily, 'someone must have told you about it, because people usually imagine that they can approach the Princess direct.'

Anwar went on his way, and found himself inside the grounds of the enormous castle. In a small pavilion in the grounds was a silent figure, sitting in contemplation. As Anwar approached him, he saw that it was the very same dervish whom he had met on the road, those many moons ago!

'As you have arrived here at last, without taking any notice of the temptations of the road' said the dervish, 'you may undergo the next test.'

He showed Anwar into a long, low meditation-hall, where rows of silent dervishes were reposing, their heads on their knees.

Anwar sat down. Then the dervishes started to perform exercises, and Anwar found himself compelled to emulate them. When this was over, he was assigned to the Master Gardener, and made to work, digging and hoeing, watering and pruning, tending plants and cutting paths, until his hands were as sore as his back ached. And all this continued for many months.

Next he was taken to the room of the Master of the Monastery, and had to go there every day for hours on end, while the great man looked at him, saying nothing. This continued for many more months.

After that, Anwar was assigned to the kitchens, where he

worked like a slave, preparing food for the hundreds of dervishes who lived in the precincts, and for the people who constantly visited the monastery, as well as for the many festivals which were conducted by the brethren.

At times Anwar felt that he was being useful, at other times that he was wasting his own time, for he thought constantly about the Princess, and also about the 'Skill that Nobody Has'.

But worse still lay before him. That was when he had no work at all to do. He was not invited to take part in the dervishes' exercises; he had no place in the kitchens, and he was not wanted in the gardens. Many other young men came and went, most of them seemed happy enough, but in conversations with them he could not learn much about the community and what the meaning was of its activities: indeed, whether there was any meaning at all.

Then, one day, after some years, Anwar was called into the presence of the Maser of the Monastery. As he reached the *hujra,* the room where the Master interviewed people, he saw that the old man was about to fall into a well which suddenly opened up in the middle of the floor. Anwar just managed to save him.

'My son,' said the sage, handing him a key, 'take this key and look after it with your life'.

Anwar went on working at the monastery until he was called into the presence of the chief of the gardeners, and he saw that a tree was toppling and was about to fall on that sage's head. Anwar just managed to prevent that happening, and saved the man's life.

'My son,' said the head gardener, 'take this crystal pebble, and guard it with your life.'

He went back to his work, and was called, after a very long time, to the presence of the chief of the kitchens. When he got there, he saw that the man was about to lift a burning-hot ladle from a pot on the fire. Anwar snatched it first, and was burned on the thumb.

'My son,' said the chief of the kitchens, 'you will now have a callous at the base of that thumb. Guard it with your life.'

After many more months in the monastery, Anwar was called into the assembly-hall, where all the dervishes were sitting having dinner. At the head of the table sat a haughty prince, with a very superior mien and dressed in glorious robes. As everyone listened, the Prince told a long and complicated story. As if it were within him, Anwar heard the Prince's voice say: 'Remember this story, and guard it with your life.'

Many days after this, Anwar was told to go to the place in the garden where he had first seen the dervish. When he got there, the old man was sitting as before, in contemplation. Raising his head, he said:

'Anwar, you are now ready to continue with your quest. You

will succeed, for I have given you the "Skill that Nobody Has".'

'But I do not understand it' said Anwar.

'If you think that you *do*,' said the sage, 'you do not. If, on the other hand, you think that you do not, you *can* exercise it without interference.'

'I still do not understand' said Anwar.

'If you had left us, you would never have learnt,' said the dervish. 'And if I drive you out, you will learn. If you try to come back, you will not learn. If you need help, I will appear.'

'Why is that?' asked Anwar, in some confusion.

'Because, apart from certain things which you have, *I* am a part of the "Skill", which cannot stay with you, so it has to be kept in me!'

So Anwar set off towards the gate of the fortress, and as he came up to the guardian of the entrance and looked at his face, he saw that he was the same man as the dervish who had been talking to him. Just outside stood the chief of the gardens, the head of the kitchen and the chief of the monastery, and all the other people whom he had met since he entered the place. Each and every one of them had the face of the dervish whom he had first met on the roadside near the top of the hill after he had left his mother's cottage!

'I shall never be able to understand this,' Anwar said to himself.

But he continued on his way.

When he looked back, he saw that the monastery was no longer there – and even the road before him had changed. Instead of leading back towards his own home, it ran in a completely different direction.

Anwar continued along it, nonetheless.

After many days he came upon a huge and brilliantly-lit city, and asked what it was.

'This,' said a passer-by, 'is the Capital of the Empire, no less.' Anwar asked him how many years had passed since the year in which he had set out, and the man looked at him oddly. 'Why, only a single year' he said. By Anwar's own reckoning, he had spent more than thirty years in that monastery, so he realised that in some strange way time was not the same everywhere.

In the centre of the city, Anwar came across a deep well, and heard cries coming from it. A rope ran down into the well, and he started to haul it up. A crowd gathered as he was straining with his utmost strength and he almost let the rope go: but he was able to sustain the terrible chafing through the callous on his thumb.

Finally, a man emerged from the well. He thanked Anwar, and said:

'You must be the Man from Afar, about whom it is prophesied

that he alone will be able to save me. I am the chief minister of His Imperial Majesty, imprisoned in the well by a Genie, and I will see that you are rewarded!'

So saying, he went his way.

Anwar was still rather surprised by this when a strange and fearsome figure jumped upon him. 'Aha!' it said, 'Son of Man, you are my prey and I shall eat you alive as I do everyone in this city whom I desire to devour. We genies are in control of the streets of the capital, and nobody can resist us except people who have earned the crystal pebble of Suleiman, son of David, which binds all the Genies on earth!'

Hearing this, Anwar snatched the pebble crystal from his pocket and held it before the genie, who immediately dissolved into flashes of fire and scuttled away, far into the distance.

No sooner had he done this, than a man on horseback came galloping up to him, and said:

'I am the Emperor's herald! It has been foretold that anyone who can rescue the Minister may be able to overcome the genies. Such a man may well have earned the key to the enchanted room in which the Princess is imprisoned. The man who can open that door is to be her husband, and to rule the realm when His Imperial Majesty is no more!'

Anwar mounted behind him, and they sped to the Palace. The man took him to a room, where Anwar fitted the key to the lock. The door swung open; and there he saw the most beautiful lady whom human eyes had ever beheld. It was, of course, the Princess, and she came forward and the pair fell in love the instant their eyes met.

And so it was that Anwar, the poor boy from the cottage in a remote province, became the husband of the Princess Salma: and Emperor, too, in the fullness of time. And he and his consort are reigning there yet.

The story which the haughty prince at the monastery table told them, they found, contained all the elements for a just, peaceful and successful rule. And whenever they, their country or their children were faced with any difficulties, they found that they had the "Skill that Nobody Has": for they were able to use their experience, the magical objects given to them, and the advice of the mysterious dervish, who always appeared and advised them when they needed him.

The Man who Went in Search of his Fate

There was once a man – and there have been many like him both before and since – who decided that he should make a change in his life. 'What is the point', he asked himself, 'of trying to do things, or letting things happen to me, if I do not know my Fate?'

If he worked against his Fate, he reasoned, he would suffer: and in the end the fate would be the same. If, on the other hand, he did nothing, his destiny would be a minor and uninteresting one: like that of the thousands of ordinary people all over the world, who had uneventful lives.

He had to start somewhere, so he sold his few possessions and began to walk along the highway which passed through his home town.

He had not been walking for very long when he came to a teahouse, where he saw a dervish sitting, talking to a number of people. The traveller – whose name was Akram – waited until the audience had gone, and then approached the man of wisdom.

'Reverend Man of the Path!' he said, 'I am in search of my Fate, and wonder whether you can suggest how I might start on this important endeavour.'

'This is easier believed possible than it is achieved' replied the dervish; 'and it would be better to ask how to *recognize* your Fate than to assume that you can do so without preparation.'

'But I am sure that I can recognize my Fate!' cried Akram, 'because it is well known that one's Fate is a reflection of oneself: and surely I can tell if I meet someone who looks like me.'

'Looking like you externally is not the same thing as being a reflection of you' said the Dervish, 'especially when, like everyone else, you have so many sides that you find it hard to see your own reflection in all its forms. The mirror of perception is as fleeting and as miscellaneous as the wavelets of the sea, each briefly shining forth with the borrowed light of the sun, as it breaks upon the seashore....'

The Dervish continued in this vein for some time, and Akram, who had met Dervishes before, stopped listening to him. He came to the conclusion that there would be nothing that he could profit from here. Still, he thought, it would be nice to have company on the journey. When the Dervish had stopped talking, Akram said: 'Mystical analogies are, of course, too deep for me to understand. But if you are travelling, might I accompany you, at least for part of the way? For I am unversed in the experiences and practices of journeying.'

The Dervish agreed, and they set off along the road.

Presently they saw a tree by the roadside, and from it was clearly to be heard a strong buzzing sound. The Dervish said: 'Put your ear to the trunk of the tree, and see what you can hear.'

Akram followed his advice and realised that the tree was hollow. Inside there was a very large number of bees.

The Dervish said: 'The bees are trapped. If you can manage to break off that branch, they will be released and will be able to escape. It might be a kindly act – and who knows where it might lead?'

Akram answered: 'Old man, you are not of this world! Has it not been said that one should not be distracted from one's objective by minor matters? Now, supposing that someone were to offer me some money for breaking the branch, I would accept, for I have no money for my journey. But to do it for nothing is absurd!'

'As you will', said the Dervish, and they continued on their way.

When it was dark they lay down to sleep. In the morning they were woken by a man going past with two large jars strapped to the sides of his donkey. He stopped to pass the time of day.

'Where are you going?' asked the Dervish.

'To market to sell this honey. It should fetch at least three pieces of gold. Yesterday I heard some bees in a hollow tree, and they seemed to want to get out. So I broke a dead branch and they swarmed. I found this huge amount of honey, and, from being a pauper, I am on the way to supporting myself!' And he went on his way.

Akram said to the Dervish: 'I should, perhaps, have got to the honey first, as you suggested. But, on the other hand, it may not have been the same tree, and in that case I would probably have been stung – and that is not the Fate I am looking for!'

The Dervish said nothing.

Further along the road they came to a bridge over a river, and stopped to admire the view. Suddenly a fish poked its head out of the water and looked at them, its mouth opening and shutting in a quite pathetic way.

'What do you think that means?' Akram asked.

The Dervish said: 'Cup your hands with interlaced fingers, and see whether you can understand the speech of the fish.'

When Akram did as the Dervish suggested, he found that he could indeed understand the fish, who was saying:

'Help me, help me!'

The Dervish called out:

'What help do you seek?'

The fish answered:

'I have swallowed a sharp stone. There is a certain herb, growing in profusion on the river-bank. If you would kindly pluck some and throw it to me, I could bring up the stone and find some relief.'

'A talking fish, indeed!' said Akram. 'I think that this is some sort of a trick of magic or ventriloquism. I refuse to make myself ridiculous. In any case, I am in search of my Fate. Dervish, if this strange happening is anything to do with you, perhaps you might care to help yonder fish yourself!'

The Dervish only said, 'No, I shall not do anything. Let us be on our way.'

Soon afterwards they entered a town and sat down in the market-place to rest. Presently a man came galloping into the square on a fine horse, obviously very excited. Dismounting, he shouted to the townspeople:

'A miracle, a miracle!'

As everyone gathered around the horseman, he said:

'I was crossing a bridge, when, believe it or not, a fish spoke to me. It asked me to throw it some herbs. I did so, and after eating them it threw up a flawless diamond as big as both my fists!'

Akram called out: 'How do you know that it is a real diamond?'

'I am a jeweller' said the man.

'How typical of life' said Akram, 'that a man of wealth should get even more, while I, unable to succour the fish because I was on important business, am forced to beg my bread in the company of a most uninteresting dervish!'

The Dervish said, 'Oh well, perhaps it was not the same fish; perhaps, indeed, that man is lying. Let us look forward and not back!'

'That is all rather like a philosopher,' said Akram, 'but much the same thoughts were in my own mind.'

They continued on their way.

The next event in their journey was when they stopped to eat beside a rock, embedded in the ground. A low humming seemed to be coming from the rock, and Akram put his ear to it. He found that the sound came from under the rock, and as he listened he could understand what it meant. It was a number of ants, and they were saying:

'If only we could move this rock, or get through it somehow, we would be able to extend our kingdom and find room for all our people. If only something could come to our aid! This hard material down here is too difficult to get through. If only someone or something would take it away!'

Akram looked at the Dervish, and said:

'The ants want the rock moved, so that they can extend their kingdom. What have I to do with ants, rocks or kingdoms? First I must find my Fate!'

The Dervish said nothing, and they continued on their way.

The following day, when they were rising from their miserable bivouac under a hedge, they heard the sound of many people coming their way, singing and shouting with glee. Presently they saw that a large band of rustics was on the road, dancing and playing fiddles and pipes, leaping and somersaulting with delight. As they passed, Akram asked one of them what had happened. The man said:

'A goatherd, believe it or not, heard some ants murmuring under a rock, in great distress. He moved it so that they could extend their nest. What do you think he found underneath? Why, a huge treasure of gold pieces! He took it and shared it with all his neighbours, and we are the lucky villagers who benefited!'

They went on their way, still delirious with delight.

The Dervish said to Akram:

'You are a fool, for you have thrice failed to do even the simplest thing that might have brought you the fortune which you desired! You are a fool, because you are even less prepared to follow your fate than all those people who just did a kind action and were not obsessed by their Fate and their personal desires! You are a fool, for you have, instead of following your fate, distanced yourself from it, by your behaviour and your failure to look at what is beneath your nose. Above all, you are a fool because you did not attend to what I am and what I have said, not said and indicated.'

Akram, like many another before and since, became enraged. He shouted at the Dervish:

'Self-satisfied and domineering know-all! Anyone can be wise, after the event! I noticed that you, a miserable and underfed wanderer on the face of the earth, did not take any advantage of the great things which you are now such an expert upon! Perhaps you can tell me why *that* is?'

'I can indeed,' replied the Dervish, 'I could not benefit myself because I had other things to do. You see, I *am* your Fate!'

Then the Dervish disappeared, and he has never been seen again: except, of course, by all the Akrams who have lived since that time, many, many years ago.

The Greed for Obstinacy

There was once an honest man, who had never, in his life, taken advantage of others. He was kind and hard-working, but he had not achieved any success in life.

This man, whose name was Singlemind, was constantly being betrayed and exploited, but this did not trouble him particularly, because – quite rightly – he knew that his own straightforwardness could not be corrupted by the villainy of others.

Singlemind practised charity and generosity and kindness to the full extent of his capacity, reposing his trust in the justice which would follow such a life: as he was convinced it must.

But he was not tranquil in mind. So he went to a Sufi and asked him what to do.

The Sufi said:

'Brother; honesty, hard work, kindness: these are all things which are of the utmost importance to humankind, if realisation is to be attained. But you must be sure that you are really honest; that you are, indeed not offsetting your generosity by an equally harmful greed for obstinacy in following your own opinions about your way of action.'

The Sufi offered him a way of observing and correcting himself, but Singlemind did not like to hear his honesty described as obstinacy, and concluded that the Sufi must be wrong.

He resolved, therefore, to make a journey to see the great saint Musa al-Kazim, to seek his advice as to how his fortune and his prospects of spiritual development might be changed.

He set off along the road.

Presently this good man, crossing a wilderness, came upon a very fierce-looking tiger, which was rolling in the dust. When he saw the traveller, the tiger stopped doing this, and said:

'Son of man, where are you going?'

Singlemind said:

'Unfortunate in my past and present, uncertain as to my future, I am seeking the great saint Musa al-Kazim, to beseech him to give me his advice.'

'I am Sher, the Tiger' said the wild beast, 'and I beg of you to ask the saint what I can do to improve my own condition, for I am miserable and out of sorts. There is something wrong with me, and I need perceptive advice.'

'Willingly', said Singlemind, and continued on his way.

In the course of time he arrived at the bank of a river, and saw a great fish, with its mouth opening and shutting, half in and half

156

out of the water.

The fish said:

'Son of man, where are you going?'

Singlemind told all that had happened.

'I am Mahi the Fish' said the fish, 'and there is something wrong with me. For some reason I cannot swim in the water, and I need some kind of help. Please ask the saint when you see him to send me advice on my problem.'

Singlemind promised to do so, and continued on his way.

After much journeying, the pilgrim came upon three men. They were wearily digging in a piece of sandy ground.

Singlemind stopped and asked them why they were labouring so hard in such an unpromising field.

'We are the three sons of a good man who has recently died,' they told him. 'Our father left us this land and told us to dig it, which is what we are doing; but it seems to us that it is so poor that nothing will ever grow on it.' They asked Singlemind what his mission was; and, when he told them, they begged him to ask for the saint's solution to their own difficulty. Singlemind willingly promised to help them in this way, and continued on his journey.

Eventually the traveller reached his destination, and found the great teacher sitting, as always, modestly and without ostentation, with a group of people who had come to learn from him.

When Singlemind approached, the saint said, 'Speak', and Singlemind said:

'I am such-and-such a man and I have come to seek your help, but before I do so I have certain representations to make, Lord, on behalf of three men, a fish and a tiger whom I met on my long journey and who may be deserving of your kindness.'

When asked to continue, he recited the difficulties which beset the men, the fish and the animal.

'Your Presence might now kindly deign to allow this unworthy person to describe his own condition, so that advice for him, too, might generously be forthcoming.'

But Musa al-Kazim said:

'My brother! Your answer has already been contained in what I have advised.'

So Singlemind retraced his steps, wondering how he could understand, from what the saint had said, how to solve his own problems.

In due time he came upon the three men, still working in the barren field. He told them:

'I have consulted the great saint, and this is his advice. "Let the three men" he said, "dig in the exact middle of the field. They will find an underground chamber with treasures which are theirs.

This is the meaning of the instruction of their father to dig the field."'

Singlemind helped the three men to follow this advice, and presently they came upon a treasure of incalculable size, together with a number of remarkable instruments which would enable people to achieve what most men call wonders, whether in the service of humanity or otherwise.

The brothers offered Singlemind his pick of gold or of the wondrous devices, but he said:

'Kind friends, I have only done my duty! All this belongs to you and I have no right to covet it. May you be in peace!' And he went on his way.

Eventually, too, he came upon the great fish who asked him if he had been able to obtain any guidance for the relief of her suffering.

'Lady fish!' said Singlemind, 'the great saint has, by his wonderful perceptions, alleviated the lot of three pauper brothers: indicating a treasure to them. His advice about your case was as follows:

"Let a blow be struck on the left side of the head of the fish, and she will thenceforward be able to swim and gambol in the water quite normally."'

The fish begged Singlemind to help, so he took his staff and struck her a blow on the place which the saint had indicated.

No sooner had he done so, than the fish slid into the water and swam, leaping and playing with unrestrained joy. Then she glided through the water to Singlemind and thanked him deeply for his help.

But Singlemind said:

'Mahi, when I struck your head, it split a lump which seems to have been upsetting your balance....'

'Yes, yes,' said Mahi, 'but that is nothing to me. I only know that I am free and well!'

Singlemind continued:

'Out of that place on your head has dropped, and is here on the bank, a diamond larger than a watermelon. Take it, or someone will surely steal it!'

'And what is that to me, a fish?' said Mahi. And she streaked away, calling down blessings upon her benefactor.

'O my sister!' Singlemind called out after her, 'you will be robbed if I leave the jewel lying here.' And he threw the huge gem into the water near where he had seen the fish disappear.

Ultimately, going his way, the traveller came to the place where the troubled tiger sat. He recited all his adventures, and the tiger asked what Musa al-Kazim had advised in his own case.

'The saint' said Singlemind, 'specifically stated that your condition could be alleviated only by devouring a fool. Do that, and you will have no further troubles.'

'And neither will you!' roared the tiger, leaping upon him.

Milk of the Lioness

There was once a time
Which was not a time
When

In a far-off kingdom all the people were waiting for the King's three daughters to be married. According to the laws of that realm, princesses of the blood royal had the right to make absolutely anyone they wished their mates, and on this occasion the ladies found it difficult to make up their minds.

Finally they asked their father to have the entire population of the kingdom paraded past them, so that they could make a choice. The first princess decided upon the tall and handsome son of one of the ministers, and the second chose the muscular and dashing son of the Emir al-Jaish, Commander of the Armies – as, indeed, everyone had always thought they would. But the third, and youngest, princess could not decide; and the endless stream of people only confused her more.

So the princess took an apple and threw it into the air, saying: 'Whoever catches this shall be my husband!'

Now it so happened that in the crowd in the public square where this was taking place there stood a young man with a limp and a hunched back, with his turban-end thrown across his face, wearing ragged clothes and walking with the aid of a staff.

This was the man who caught the apple, and who dragged himself to the platform where the royal family sat, to claim his prize.

The crowd cheered, more because of habit than anything else, for inwardly they did not feel happy that such a man should become one of the ruling house. The son of the minister and the military commander's son muttered to themselves and to each other. And the King said to his minister:

'The royal word may never be withdrawn, so let the stupid girl

159

have the clown or buffoon, or whatever he is. At least I have two stalwart and reliable sons-in-law!'

What nobody knew at that time, of course, was that the youth was only pretending to be what he seemed to be. The lameness was affected and the crouched posture was assumed, and he covered the lower part of his face because he did not want to be recognised. He was a fugitive Hashemite Emir, concealing himself from persecution.

All three girls were married and, since the young prince, Ibn Haidar, did not reveal himself, he and his bride were banished to a stable to live, by her enraged father.

Even his own wife did not realise who Ibn Haidar was, but she loved him, whatever he looked like, and both of them accepted the life of poverty and ostracism which was their lot.

Ibn Haidar used to walk, in the evenings, out of the city and contemplate in a small cave where nobody else ever seemed to go. After some months he met an old man, who said to him:

'Son of the Lion (which is what Ibn Haidar means) you must wait until the Day of Lion Milk. When you hear of this, you should take action towards the restitution.' And the old man handed him a clear stone. 'Rub this stone in your right hand and think of a very small, broken coin, and you can summon the Magical Charcoal Mare.'

So saying, he went on his way.

Now it came to pass that the King was engaged in war, and he rode out with his armies, his two valiant sons-in-law and his commanders to engage the enemy. Naturally, they left the lame and misshapen Ibn Haidar behind. They fought many battles, but at last it seemed that the invaders of the country were gaining the upper hand. At this point Ibn Haidar felt the stone grow hot in his pocket, and he took it out, remembering the broken coin. As he turned it in his fingers, a splendid, charcoal-coloured mare appeared. It said to him:

'My Lord, put on the accoutrements in my saddle-bags: we ride to war!'

When he was fully arrayed in knightly mail, the youth leapt upon the back of the horse, and she flew through the skies until they reached the battlefield. The mysterious knight fought from dawn to dusk, until the enemy were routed, almost entirely through his bravery. The King rode up to him and threw his own Kashmir shawl around his neck, saying:

'Blessings upon you, lordly one, for you have aided the good and opposed evil, and we are eternally in your debt.'

But Ibn Haidar said nothing. He bowed to the King, raised his lance in salutation, and, spurring the magical mare into the clouds, returned home.

When the warriors arrived back at the capital, they were full of tales of the mysterious knight who had saved them, and spoke of him as the 'Black Knight of Heaven'. The King said, again and again:

'Would that I had a son-in-law like that!'

Ibn Haidar, of course, continued to be the butt of jokes, a curiosity and a nonentity, even though he was the husband of a princess.

After some months, the young man was sitting in his stable when he felt the stone grow hot again. When he took it out and rubbed it, not forgetting to think of the coin, the horse appeared and said:

'On my back! We have work to do.'

The horse took him to the King's castle, through a window into the royal bedchamber, where Ibn Haidar was just in time to snatch and kill a snake which was about to strike at the head of the King. At that moment the monarch awoke and saw what had happened. In the gloom he could not see who his deliverer was, but he took off his priceless ruby ring and handed it to him, saying:

'I owe you my life, whoever you are. This ring shall be a token for you.'

Ibn Haidar took the ring and his steed flew him back to the miserable stable.

His life continued as before for a number of months, when the stone called him again, and he summoned the horse.

'Put on the robe and turban in my saddle-bags' cried the mare, 'for we have work to do.'

The animal carried Ibn Haidar to the King's throne-room, where a man had just been condemned to death. The executioner had already spread his leather carpet to catch the blood and was awaiting the royal signal with sword upraised. At the sight of the black mare with the robed figure upon it, everyone stiffened, as if made of wood. Ibn Haidar waited, and within a few moments there was a commotion at the throne-room door. A man had arrived with proof that the condemned man was innocent. Everyone at the court was amazed, and the King said to the mysterious apparition:

'Blessings upon him who intervenes for justice! Take this sword of mine as a token.'

Without a word Ibn Haidar girded on the sword and the mare took him back, through the clouds, to his stable.

Nothing of great importance happened for many more months, until, one day, the King became ill. It was as if the whole world had darkened, and people went about the streets as if in mourning. Even the animals were silent, the trees drooped, and

161

the sun itself seemed dim. No doctor could find out what ailed the ruler, until the greatest of them all, the Hakim Al Hukuma, the Doctor of all Doctors, pronounced:

'This illness is to be cured only by a draught of the milk of a lioness, brought from the Land of Not-Being.'

Immediately the two sons-in-law of the King offered themselves for the task, and rode out from the palace in full determination to earn the glory of saving their lord and master.

After many days they arrived at a crossroads, where a wise man sat. The road branched into three highways, and the two men were unable to decide which one to follow. They explained their mission to the wise man, who said:

'These three roads have names. The first is called "The Road of Those who do as We do, the Bond of Blood". The second is called "The Road of Those who think as We do, the Bond of Decision", and the third is called "The Road of Truth".'

The first son-in-law said:

'I shall take the Road of Blood, for it is through kinship with his Majesty that I am here.' He spurred his horse on its way.

The second son-in-law cried:

'I shall take the Road of Decision, for decisiveness is my way.' And he galloped away.

Presently the first young man came to a man at the entrance to a city, and asked him where he was.

'You are at the gateway to "The Land of Not-Being"' answered the man, 'but you cannot enter it until you have played chess with me.' They sat and played, and the young man lost. He lost his horse, his armour, his money and, finally, his freedom.

The other man took him into the city and sold him to a cooked-meat seller, and there he stayed for many days.

As to the second youth, he, too, arrived at the gateway of the city, and the same thing happened to him. He was taken into the city and sold as a slave to a sweetmeat-seller.

After several months, when there was no sign of the return of the champions, Ibn Haidar felt the stone grow hot in his pocket, and he summoned the black mare.

'The time is now!' she said, 'jump on my back.'

He followed the same road until he reached the spot where the wise man sat, and told him his mission.

The man gave him his choice of the three roads and Ibn Haidar said at once:

'I choose the "Road of Truth".' He was about to continue on his way when the wise man said:

'You have made the right choice. Continue: but when you get to the chess-player, challenge him to combat rather than playing with him.'

Ibn Haidar went on, and when the chess-player asked him to play he drew his sword and cried:

'For Truth, not tricks! Face reality, not token battle: see before you him who says, "O people of Hashim!"' For that was his battle-cry.

The chess-player surrendered without a fight, and told Ibn Haidar what had happened to his brothers-in-law.

He took him into the city and showed him where the lionesses were kept. After outwitting the guards and taming the beasts, the young man took three flasks of milk. He put one in each saddle-bag and one in his turban, as a precaution against their being broken or lost.

Now he went to the sweetmeat-seller and the vendor of cooked meats and brought back the other two young men, although they did not recognise him in his knightly garb. That night, however, the pair of them – who knew that he had the lioness's milk – stole a flask each and fled the city under cover of darkness.

Ibn Haidar gave them time to reach the palace and then mounted the magical mare which, faster than an arrow, carried him to the very sick-room of the ailing King.

As he alighted from his horse and strode to the bed, the assembled doctors and courtiers, and the brothers-in-law, were awestricken at his appearance. As the turban he wore the Kashmir shawl of the King, on his finger was the great ruby ring, and at his side hung the royal sword.

'Here is the milk of the Lionesses of the Land of Not-Being,' he said, as he approached the bed.

'But you are too late!' everyone cried. The King said:

'These sons-in-law of mine have brought back the milk, but it does me no good.'

Ibn Haidar said:

'That is because they stole it from me, who obtained it: and all special virtue flees from something obtained by theft. Here is the third flask. Take a draught, O King!'

As soon as the King had swallowed a little of the milk, he sat up, completely cured.

The King said:

'Whence do you come, and who are you, and why do you help me?'

The young man said:

'The three questions are one question, and an answer to the first is an answer to all; the answer to the second is an answer to all; the answer to the third is an answer to all.'

The King did not understand.

163

'Very well,' said Ibn Haidar, 'I am the man who lives in the stable, which means that I am your son-in-law, which is why I help you.'

And that was how Ibn Haidar came to inherit the crown of the kingdom, when the King was taken, in the fullness of time, on his longest journey.

The Spirit of the Well

There was once a couple who lived in a small village and who used to argue all the time.

One day the wife became so enraged with something said by her foul-mouthed husband that she clipped him around the ear, and he tumbled into their deep well.

Now at the bottom of that well, as is often the case, lived a Genie; and he was an unusually fierce and abominable one. As soon as the husband saw him, he started to scream and shout, to pull him about, and to shower upon him such abuse as he had not heard since the days of the great King Suleiman, son of David (upon whom Peace!) until the Genie, affronted and affrighted, was forced to rise from his dwelling. This was how he came to ascend into the sky, towering over the terrified wife as she stood looking down into the depths of the well.

'Miserable woman!' roared the Genie, as soon as he saw her, 'Who is responsible for flinging that unbelievably appalling human into my well, disturbing my peace and causing me to flee from my home of the past ten thousand years?'

'What about me?' asked the woman, '*I* have had to live with that man for two decades, and *you* cannot stand him for two minutes!'

'You unfortunate creature!' cried the Genie, for he was not without some better feelings and the howls of the frightful husband were still ringing in his ears, 'I certainly do see your point of view.'

'Well' said the woman, 'since I do not want him out of the well, and you do not want to go back, you might as well come along with me to the city, for I have decided to walk there to see what life might have in store for me. To stay here would be to starve, and in any case I want to get as far away from that man as possible.'

The Genie agreed, and they set off along the road, chatting

amicably together.

Presently the Genie said:

'How are you going to live in the big city?'

'Something will turn up' said the woman.

'My suggestion' said the Genie, 'is this: the king has a daughter.
I will enter into her brain and possess her. Then you come along
and cast me out, and the king will reward you.'

'That is an excellent idea' said the woman.

'But there is one proviso' said the Genie. 'That is that you will
only use the word of exorcism once, otherwise I will always be at
your mercy.'

'All right' said the woman.

The Genie sped on ahead and drove the princess completely
mad. She writhed and she cried, she cursed and she threw herself
about, and everyone soon realised that a genie of some kind had
entered into her.

As soon as the woman reached the town, she met people who
told her the terrible story. 'The king,' they added, 'has promised
illimitable gold to anyone who can cure her, and to hang anyone
who falsely pretends to be able to do so.'

As soon as she reached the main market of the city, the woman
began calling out: 'Genies cast out! The world's greatest caster-out
has arrived! Bring out your begenied people, I shall cast them out!'

Almost at once she was seized by the royal guards and taken to
the king. The princess was brought forward, grimacing and
howling – and the woman, using the word which the Genie had
told her, cast him out.

Of course the king, as well as the princess, was delighted by
this, and they rewarded the exorcist with as much gold as she
wanted, and she established herself in a palace of her own, which
rivalled that of the monarch himself.

But the Genie was not finished. After a few months' roaming
about, unable to go home to his well and feeling the need to do
some further mischief, he found himself back in the selfsame city
and, almost without noticing what he was doing, entered into the
princess's mother, the queen.

The king immediately called the exorcist woman and commanded:

'Cast out this demon at once, or I shall kill you!'

Since it was a matter of her life or the Genie, she went to the
queen's bedside and whispered the magic word. With a roar and a
rush, the infuriated spirit stood beside her in the form of an ox
with a snake's head, breathing out fumes and rolling his eyes.

'By the Great King Suleiman, son of David, on whom Peace!' he
roared, 'I shall seize you for this, and you will never be able to cast

me out, for you will be too begenied to remember the magic word!'

'My dear friend,' said the clever woman, 'if you dare to do that, I shall immediately return to my husband, and you and I will have to endure him for the rest of your time inhabiting me!'

And, at the frightful prospect, the Genie took flight, roared away – and has never been seen again.

The Princess of the Water of Life

Once upon a time, when there was not a time, in the country of No-Place-At-All, there lived, all alone in a small hut, a poor girl whose name was Jayda.

Walking in the woods one day, Jayda saw that a colony of bees had abandoned their honey, and she decided to collect it.

'I shall take it to market, and sell it, and try to improve my life with the money I shall get' she told herself.

Jayda ran home and brought a jar, which she filled with the honey. But she did not know that the reason for her poverty was a malefic Jinn, who tried all he could to prevent her from making anything a success.

The Jinn woke up as something told him that Jayda was starting to do something useful, and he rushed to the spot, intent on causing trouble. As soon as he saw Jayda with the honey, he turned himself into a branch attached to a tree, and jogged her arm, so that the jar fell and broke, and the honey all seeped into the ground.

The Jinn, still in the form of the branch, laughed and laughed, swinging back and forth with glee. 'This will infuriate her!' he cackled to himself.

But Jayda just looked at the honey and said to herself:

'Never mind, the ants will eat the honey, and perhaps something may come of it.' She had seen a line of ants whose scouts were already tasting the honey to see if it was useful to them. As she started to walk through the woods back to her hut, Jayda noticed that a man on horseback was coming towards her.

When he was only a few yards away, he idly raised his whip and struck at a tree in passing. Jayda saw that it was a mulberry tree, and the blow had made the ripe fruit shower onto the ground. She thought, 'That's a good idea. I'll collect mulberries and take them to market to sell. Perhaps something will come of it.'

The Jinn saw her collecting the fruit and laughed to himself. When Jayda had filled her basket, he turned himself into a donkey and followed quietly behind her on her way to market.

When she sat down to rest, the Jinn in the form of a donkey edged up to her, nuzzling her arm. Jayda stroked his nose: and then the horrid creature suddenly rolled over onto the basket of mulberries, crushing them to pulp. The juice ran all over the road, and the Jinn-ass gleefully galloped away into the bushes.

Jayda looked at the fruit in dismay. At that moment, however, the Queen had been approaching, on her way to the capital.

'Stop at once!' she ordered her palanquin-bearers, 'for that poor girl has lost everything. Her donkey has squashed her fruit and run off. She will be ruined if we do not help her.'

So the Queen took Jayda with her in her palanquin, and they became fast friends. She gave Jayda a house and Jayda soon became a successful merchant in her own right.

When he saw how well Jayda was getting on, the Jinn had a good look at her house to see what he could do to ruin her. He realised that she kept all her goods in a warehouse behind the house: so he set fire to the house and goods, and the place was burned to the ground in almost less time than it takes to tell.

Jayda had run out of the house when she smelt the smoke, and looked at the ruins with sorrow. Then she noticed that a line of tiny ants was forming, and then that they were carrying their stocks of corn, one grain at a time, from beneath the house to a place of greater safety.

To help them, Jayda lifted a large stone covering their nest. Beneath it gushed a spring of water.

As Jayda tasted it, the people of the city gathered around her and cried:

'The Water of Life! This is what has been foretold!'

They told her that it had been prophesied that one day after a fire and after many disasters a spring would be found by a young girl who disregarded calamities. This would be the last fountain of life.

And that is how Jayda became known as the Princess of the Water of Life, which she still tends, and which can be drunk, to give immortality to those who find it by disregarding calamity.

Fahima and the Prince

There was once, in the city of Basra, a very beautiful and intelligent girl, expert at solving conundrums and usually able to predict people's actions far better than they themselves ever could.

Her name, in fact, was Fahima, 'The Understander'. She had inherited a large fortune, and all the young men of the city – as well as a number of older ones – wanted to marry her, most of them hoping to get hold of her money. Women, too, sought her friendship. Those who did not want her wealth were curious about the source and action of her remarkable cleverness: and so Fahima was always besieged by suitors, well-wishers, idlers and people trying to sell her things.

Fahima shut herself away and very sensibly made it difficult for people to get to know her. Then one day when she was standing for a moment on the turret of her castle, briefly lit by the rays of the sun, a certain prince came by and saw her. He decided that he would marry her.

The prince camped outside the castle and laid siege to the fair lady. He sang her songs, played on the lute, displayed his manly figure in a great variety of splendid robes, and sent her poems and messages. In between all these activities, he broke off to go hunting, withdrew to practise sword-fighting, rode into the city to inspect the latest cargoes from distant lands, and generally acted as princes of that time usually did.

Fahima, as we know, was wise; and she both liked what she had seen and heard of the prince, and understood him better than he understood himself. One day, therefore, when she went out of the castle and found herself seized and borne back to the prince's own castle, she was not as surprised as some people might have been. When he threw her into a dungeon without any discussion, she realised that he had done this because he had convinced himself that she would not marry him until he had shown his assertiveness and power; because as you will have gathered, he was in the habit of coming to conclusions about situations without sufficient reflection.

After some days the prince went to Fahima's prison and called through the bars:

'Fahima, I want to marry you. I have money, I am young and strong and handsome, and I have you in my power, and can do anything I like with you. Moreover, I can please you and make you

168

an interesting and devoted husband.'

Fahima answered:

'Not by money, not by honey
Not by guile, nor by wile;
Not through boasting, or even roasting!'

Day after day the prince went to the dungeon, and a similar kind of conversation took place. He suggested all the reasons why he thought she should marry him, and she rejected them all. Finally other things began to occupy his mind. After some months he decided to go to Baghdad for a time, and word of this came to Fahima through the gossip of her jailer.

But Fahima had not been idle. All that time she had been tunnelling, and she now had a means of escape to the outside world.

As soon as the prince left, Fahima went down her secret passage to freedom and, hiring the fastest horses in Basra, made her way to the capital, arriving long before the indolent prince, who made his way there in state and with many halts to have food prepared and for all kinds of other reasons.

When the prince arrived in Baghdad he visited friends, he went hunting with hawks and gave lavish entertainment, and generally comported himself as princes did in those days.

One day, strolling past a luxurious mansion, he saw a beautiful girl standing by a window. He thought: 'That lovely creature is almost exactly like Fahima of Basra!' And well he might, for it was the very same girl, who had established herself in Baghdad for the very purpose of meeting the prince.

The prince instantly contrived to meet the lady and asked her to marry him. She agreed, they were wed, Fahima became a princess, and she gave birth in due course to a baby girl. The prince was delighted, of course.

After a time, however, he decided to go on his travels again; and he journeyed to Tripoli. Fahima, leaving her child with a trusted servant, went there too, and took a sumptuous house. Again the prince saw her, again he found that he wanted to marry her – thinking that she was another woman – and again they were married. This time they had a baby boy, and the prince was, of course, delighted.

When wanderlust again arose in the prince's breast, he took ship to Alexandria where, needless to say, Fahima also went, and everything went as before. The prince saw her, asked her to marry him, married her, and they had another child.

After a year or two, the prince felt homesick for Basra and he embarked for that city, leaving his wife, as he thought, in Alexandria. Fahima chartered a faster ship and arrived back in time to be sitting in her dungeon when the prince went to see her.

When he saw her, the prince began, for the first time, to feel remorse and distress. 'Ah, Fahima!' he cried, 'I would still like to marry you, and I have treated you badly, leaving you imprisoned here for so many years. But I am not really the same man. I am even worse. I have done things which I should not have done, and I am unworthy of you, and, indeed, of the others about whom you know nothing!'

Fahima said:

'Are you prepared to tell me the truth about what has happened while you have been away?'

'I might as well,' said the prince, 'but it will make little difference. Clever as you are, even you would not be able to think of a solution to my problems, brought about by foolishness and lack of reflection.'

Fahima said:

'If you tell me the whole story, omitting no single detail, I might be able to suggest something.'

The prince then related how he had met and married beautiful girls in Baghdad, Tripoli and Alexandria, how he had three children, and how he wished he had acted differently.

'Were it not for me,' said Fahima, 'you would have done all these things in an irrevocable form. If that had happened, you would not have been able to undo your folly, and others would have been harmed through your own selfishness. As it happens, I am able to unravel the thread for you.'

'What has been done cannot be undone!' cried the prince; 'and, as for the rest of your speech, I do not understand it at all.'

'Go to your drawing-room' said Fahima, 'and wait there until someone is announced, someone whom you must instantly have admitted to your presence.'

The prince did as she asked, and in an hour or so, dressed in all her finery and leading their three children, Fahima appeared at the castle gate.

It was some time before the prince could understand that the four women were in fact one, and that all of his three children had the same mother. But, when he realised what Fahima had done, in spite of what he had done to her, he was overwhelmed with joy, and became a completely reformed character. They all lived happily ever afterwards.

Salik and Kamala

There was once a youth named Salik, who lived in a city ruled by a stern King, whose edicts were so strict and so all-encompassing that people obeyed them without thinking, and regarded them almost as laws of nature.

The King had a daughter, whose name was Kamala – which means perfection; and she was indeed perfection in every sense. She was intelligent, beautiful and wise; and there was a law that she was not to be seen, or spoken to, or even thought about too much. Of course there were people who saw her sometimes; and some people had to speak to her, from among her servants; but in general people thought about her so little, and about the dangers of thinking about her so much, that many of the citizens almost feared her name.

One day, however, Salik was walking by the seashore when he glimpsed the Princess coming out of the sea after her morning bathe, and he fell in love with her; or he thought that he had, for the many sensations of attraction, fear and curiosity struggled within him.

Salik spoke to his parents of what he had seen, and they were terrified, and advised him to forget the matter. 'We can have a good enough life here if we obey the King's orders and serve him within his commands' said his father, who was a respected and learned man.

But Salik began to feel, more and more strongly, that he would like to see the Princess again, and he took to haunting the seashore and wandering in the woods near the city, in the hope of glimpsing her.

Now the Princess, for her part, had also espied Salik, and she fell in love with him. She confided in an old woman who visited the palace as a pedlar, and the crone sought out Salik, as she went from door to door.

One day, after visiting hundreds of houses, the hag found herself face to face with Salik.

'My child', she said, 'the Princess loves you, and you must now do your own part. In spite of what the King says you must win your way through to the girl; and is she not more beautiful than the moon?'

Salik, of course, was astonished and delighted that such as he, an insignificant youth, should love and be loved by the Princess, and he promised the old woman that he would find a way to meet her, and by seeking her out in spite of dangers, would prove his

171

love.

Encouraged by the exciting message, Salik felt fear of the King's wrath far less than before, and he quitted his house to walk through the city while he made plans to meet his beloved.

He had not gone far when he came across a crowd, surrounding a man on a whipping-block. 'What is happening?' asked Salik.

'This man', the people told him, 'spoke in terms of admiration about the Princess. Naturally, the King is having him punished.'

As he looked at the horror of the flayed flesh, Salik's heart sank, and he feared that such a fate might be his if he persisted in his secret desires.

But, as he continued on his way, his admiration and determination returned, and he started to lay plans to meet the girl.

Then he turned a corner, and he found a crowd of people jeering at a man who was being evicted from his shop. They threw mud at him and as the soldiers of the King flung all his goods on the street, the people stole them.

When he asked what was happening, the people told Salik:

'Thus disgraced are those who covet the daughter of our most wise and powerful master the King. This man made up a poem about her.'

Salik's heart turned to water, and he saw what the penalty might be for him; but then his resolve returned and he continued on his way.

Presently, he saw a man looking towards the sky as he walked: and suddenly the King's Guards appeared, seized him and carried him off. When Salik asked bystanders what crime the man had committed, they said:

'Looking upwards is a crime. Such a person might one day find himself gazing towards the Princess's turret window, so he has to be stopped.'

So Salik, to protect himself, started to walk with his gaze fixed on the ground. He had been walking along in this way for some time when he saw the old crone beckoning to him.

'Young man,' she said, 'you are not doing anything about the Princess, and if you love her as she loves you, you must take some steps towards it, in case she becomes disenchanted with you.'

'I think that I have made a start' said Salik.

'And how is that?' asked the woman.

'First, I have said nothing about her to anyone except my parents. Second, I have composed no poetry about her.'

'Then,' said the old woman, 'why are you looking at the ground?'

'I was just going to tell you, hag' said Salik, 'that I was protecting myself by not looking up at windows.'

'You foolish creature!' cried the woman, 'do you not know that

172

there is a law and custom that people do not look at the ground, in case this means that they are seeking the Princess's footsteps?'

And she went on her way.

Suddenly, as he was passing a house, thinking only of the Princess, Salik heard a weeping and wailing from within. He rushed inside, calling out, in his obsession, 'Is she dead? Oh, is she dead? Let me see her for the last time!'

The mourners looked at him and thought that he must be a madman.

'Young man', they said, 'we grieve because one of our relatives has died. But you, a stranger, have no right to burst in here in this unseemly manner. Besides, it is not a woman who has died; it is a man.'

Salik went on his way.

Presently he found himself at a crossroads where a venerable sage sat, a Sufi teacher, with half-closed eyes. This man said to him:

'Salik, my friend, you have little time left to find the Princess. You have been looking up and looking down; you have been following your own inclinations and exciting yourself over a death. Now it is time for you to find out whether you really seek the Princess or whether you seek to avoid the manners of the people of this town.'

Salik cried out:

'But what can I do?'

'What you can do is to take the straight road' said the Sufi; 'but, because of what people are doing and having done to them, you cannot make this choice. Come with me.'

He took Salik by the arm and together they walked along the road until they arrived at the palace of the King. 'Are you afraid of death?' asked the old man. 'Are you afraid of loss of goods and disgrace?' he continued; 'are you afraid of advice and help?'

'I only do what others do, and avoid what others avoid,' answered Salik.

'Only' said the sage, 'what *some* others do and *some* others do not do; and this you think is the behaviour of "all others".'

They entered the palace and the Sufi guided Salik to the throne-room where the King sat in Court.

'Your Majesty' said the sage, 'this is the youth Salik, who has feared and who has imagined, and now he has come to you to ask for the hand of your daughter, the Princess Kamala, in marriage.'

'I rule,' said the King, 'over this area where danger is every-where, where all must die, where people are constantly disapproved. Those who fear danger unnecessarily, who fear death, who cannot endure disapproval, remain slaves. Are they

173

worthy of the daughters of those who rule?'

'If your Majesty's laws say that I must now die, then kill me!' said Salik. 'If you disapprove of my ambition, disgrace me! All I now know is that I want to marry the Princess.'

And that is how Salik married Kamala and became, in his turn, ruler of the kingdom. And Salik, of course, means 'Seeker', while Kamala is the word for 'Perfection'; so he attained her only after he had put aside those things which stood between them.

When the Devil Went to Amman

Once upon a time there was an old woman, going from the country to the city of Amman, to visit her grandson. It was summer, and on the hot and dusty road she came upon a tired-looking but rather sinister man in a black cloak.

'Good morning!' she said, for she had nothing better to do, and country-people always salute one another.

'And a *bad* morning to you!' he answered.

'That's a fine way to speak to people,' said the old woman, 'and what kind of a man are you that you say such things to the children of Adam?'

'I hate the Children of Adam – and I talk like that because I am the Devil' he snarled.

The old woman was not at all afraid. 'And why should you be on the road to the great city?' she asked.

'Ah,' said the Devil, 'there is plenty for me to do in such a place.'

'You don't look much of a devil to me' said the old woman; 'why, I believe that I could match anything that you could do, any day!'

'Very well,' snapped the Devil, 'I'll give you three days in Amman, and if you can do worse things than me, I'll leave the town alone for the rest of my days...'

So the bargain was struck, and the two of them arrived together in the city.

'When are you going to start?' the Devil asked, for he was longing to see some wickedness.

'I'll start right away, and you can watch me, providing, that is,

174

that you can make yourself invisible' she told him.

'Like this?' he asked, and she realised that he had made himself disappear from sight, though she could feel his hot breath on her ear. 'Now get on with it,' he rasped.

The old woman made her way to the shop of one of the biggest merchants of fine cloth in the city, and sat down at the entrance, asking the merchant to bring out some really fine silk.

'It would have to be something really unusual', she said. 'My grandson is in love with a certain married woman and he wants to give her a present that she will never forget, to soften her heart towards him. She has said that she will yield, if only she can have a bolt of the very finest silk that can be found.'

'Why you want it is no business of mine, so please do not tell me any details,' replied the man. 'But I have here, as it happens, a bolt of the very finest cloth in all the world. Until the other day there were two bolts of it. Then I sold one to the Royal Palace, so you can imagine the quality.'

While she was examining it, the crone said:

'Now this is very expensive stuff, and I expect that I shall buy it. How is it that you are not treating me with the respect which is due to a valued customer?'

'What do you mean?' asked the merchant.

'Well, at the very least, you should call for a pipe for me, so that I have a smoke while I am deciding....'

The merchant immediately called for a pipe, which was brought, with charcoal burning well in the container on top of it. He also placed near her a plate of sticky pastry baklawas.

Mumbling to herself, the old woman fingered the cloth and ate the pastry, and in between she puffed at the tube of the pipe. Suddenly the merchant noticed with dismay that she had smeared some of the honey from her fingers on the priceless cloth, and – even worse – she had tilted the pipe and allowed a piece of glowing charcoal to fall on the silk, burning a hole right through it.

'Ayee! You foolish crone!' he cried, 'you are ruining the cloth!'

'Not at all. All that I have to do is to cut it in a certain way and thus eliminate the stain and the hole' she said; 'because I am buying it, anyway. How much did you say it was?'

'A hundred pounds' he said, expecting to conclude the bargain at fifty. But she immediately accepted without a quibble, paid him the money, and left the shop.

As she went down the street, the devil whispered at her elbow, 'I don't call that much of a trick: true, you gave him a small shock, but you overpaid him and he thinks that you are a fool. He is more of a devil than you are!'

'Be silent!' hissed the old woman, 'and have some patience, for goodness' sake. Watch what I do next.'

So saying, she began to ask questions of people in a café, until she had found out the address of the home of the cloth merchant.

It was a large and opulent-looking house, and the crone stood outside intoning prayers, and then knocked on the door.

The merchant's wife called out:

'Who is there and what do you want?'

'Peace be upon you, magnanimous lady!' the old crone called up to her window 'know that I am only a poor woman from the country, come to visit my son. I am caught here in the street at the time of my special prayers, and I cannot find a quiet, clean place in which to say them.'

So the merchant's wife invited the pious lady in, and showed her into the large sitting-room on the ground floor.

'Kind lady,' wheezed the aged one, 'as one last favour, I beg that I might be lent a prayer-rug, on which to kneel.'

The merchant's wife looked around and brought out her husband's *sajjadah* from his room and handed it to her.

The old woman pretended to say her prayers while the other woman withdrew to her own quarters. Then she rolled up the carpet, with the cloth which she had bought inside it, and handed the rug back with a thousand words and gestures of thanks and of humility.

When she left the house, the Devil again angrily asked her what kind of play-acting this was, but she gave him the same answer as before.

When the merchant returned home that evening and took out his rug to say his prayers, out dropped the roll of cloth. It had the same mark and the same hole as the one which he had sold to the crone. The bolt, he remembered, which was a gift to a married woman who would yield to her grandson in return for it. . . .

His own wife! The merchant was blazing with fury. As the Devil invisibly stood by, he turned his wife out of the house, refusing to listen to anything she said.

'This is more like it!' the Devil chuckled to himself. The old woman followed the distracted wife, to see where she went, and saw that she ran to the house of her cousin, where she threw herself upon a bed, crying bitterly, and refusing to explain anything to anyone.

The following morning the old woman went to see her grandson, a lusty youth who was no better than he should be. 'Come, my fine young fellow' she said to him, 'I am going to introduce you to a fine and intelligent lady, who is lonely and distraught. . . .'

She took the youth to the house where the merchant's wife was resting and – profiting from the anxiety and confusion of the lady, insisted that the two should remain together. Such was the bewilderment of the pair that they simply sat in the room, looking at one another, as though mesmerised by the crone.

Now the ancient hag sped to the merchant's shop. As soon as he saw her, he started to cry and beat his breast, calling out, 'O crone of ill-fortune! Why should you choose me to be the instrument of the seduction of my own wife, by your infernal, misbegotten grandson! Why have you come back to torment me? Begone, before I kill you!' And there was much more in the same vein.

The old woman stood her ground until the merchant was somewhat out of breath, and then she said:

'O King of Merchants! I really have no idea as to the reason for your words. I only come to say that I am here to ask for the return of my silk which I seem to have left, by some oversight, at your house. But there is nobody at home!'

The Devil was wheezing into her ears as he heard this, suffocating with stifled laughter.

'What!' shouted the merchant; 'Do you mean to tell me that it is not my wife who was to be suborned by means of the silk?'

'Certainly not – all that happened was that I chanced upon your house when I was looking for a place to pray, and negligently left the material there . . .'

Almost beside himself with the remains of his fury, with grief and anguish at the injustice which he had done to his wife, the merchant cried:

'O that I could get my beloved wife back!'

'Now' said the hag, 'I may be able to help you there.'

'If only you can get her back, kind woman' said the merchant, 'I would give you a thousand pounds, and in gold!'

'Done!' screamed the harridan, and skipped out of the shop.

'Don't tell me that you are going to do someone a good turn, you crazy old jade' rustled the Devil into her ear.

'Get away from me, you fool, so that a real expert can get to work!' screeched the hag, while a look of ultimate cunning spread across her features.

The Devil lurked beside her as she made her way to the prison where her grandson and the merchant's wife were held.

As soon as she saw the jailer at the prison gate, the hag started to keen and sway:

'O, most noble of all guardians of the justice of the King! To think that in my old age I should have been brought to this. . . . Yet perhaps, good Sir, kind gentleman, illustrious one, you may be able to help me. . . .'

She held out a golden sovereign, and the jailer looked at her with greater interest.

'What do you want?' he gruffed.

'Only that I should be allowed to enter for a few small moments to see my grandson, who has, quite rightly of course, been locked up in your charge, brave custodian of justice!'

'Well, then, if you have another coin to match that one, something might be arranged' said the man.

Quick as a flash, she passed him two gold pieces, and he let her in.

As soon as she reached the dungeon where the accused pair were locked in adjoining cells, she went to the one where the merchant's wife was and unbolted the door.

'Hurry and take my old robe and veil and leave me yours. Leave this jail pretending to be me and join your husband: that is, if you are willing to reward me for your deliverance and his forgiveness.'

'I have a thousand gold pieces at home, would that be enough?' cried the distraught woman. 'That will do nicely; but mind you do not go back on your word, or I shall tell the merchant that you really were guilty after all!' croaked the hag.

So the merchant's wife put on the crone's clothes, and the crone dressed herself as the wife, and she and the lad were left in the dungeon while the merchant's wife rushed home to her delighted husband.

That evening, according to law, the examining magistrate visited the gaol to see whether there was real cause for the incarceration of its inmates. When he arrived at the cell where the hag was he asked:

'Why are these people being kept here?'

'They were seized on an accusation of immorality, my lord Judge' said the jailer.

The hag threw off her veil and whined:

'Noble Judge! I am a woman of ninety years of age, and this is my grandson, who is hardly more than sixteen years old! Here are papers to prove it. We were sitting talking innocently together when some miscreant denounced us to the police on this absurd charge. Please, noble Sir, order our release at once, for we have indeed suffered enough!'

The magistrate, furious, turned upon the jailer and the policeman in charge of the case, and roared:

'Is this the way in which justice is being done in our land? Discharge this innocent old lady and her charming grandson at once!' To the escort he said:

'Give the jailer and the policeman ten strokes with your switch!'

As the old woman and her grandson walked away from the jailhouse, they came upon the Devil.

'I'm off', he said, 'for after seeing such a performance I know that

178

I cannot compete!' And he opened his wings and flew straight back to Jehennum.

And that is why you never come across any devilment in Amman, since the old lady has not tried her hand at it again.

The Robe

There was once a man who made up his mind that he would deceive a King. He laid his plans deeply, and this is what he did:

He was living in a small town, like many a small town of today, where people find it easy to acquire a reputation for goodness through outward acts and benign faces. He started to speak more quietly, to dress more simply, and to grow his beard long. His prayers were endless, and people began to regard him as a man of worth and weight. These people, of course, had not heard the saying, 'The best of men is he whose beard is shortest, and the worst of men is he who makes his public prayers long.'

After dropping some small hints, this man, whose name was Shatir, built a small hut with two doors on a high place, and used to visit it frequently, dressed in a single sheet, intoning prayers and invocations.

When people asked him what he was doing, Shatir only answered, 'I am calling upon the Celestial Powers and live in the hope that they may answer me, if I am ever to become sufficiently worthy, though I have great doubt about this.'

Thus he gained a reputation of piety and humility. People started to visit his shrine, and to stand outside, while the pious voice of Shatir was heard from within.

After a number of months, people noticed that Shatir spent more and more time in his retreat. When they stood outside, they heard voices, as if Shatir was conversing with someone. The news spread throughout the town.

One day, when he was in the town, Shatir visited the largest merchant's shop and stopped to converse. This merchant was inquisitive and greedy, and he plied Shatir with questions, but the sage instead asked about the price of certain valuable cushions and a fine carpet which adorned the place.

The merchant's curiosity increased. Why, he asked himself, did Shatir want such things? How could he ever afford to buy them, even if he did want them? What were they for?

Then Shatir asked how much the goods would be if he were simply to hire them for a time, and whether there were any finer

179

cushions or carpets to be had in all the town.

Finally the merchant said, 'Friend Shatir. I know that you are a good man, and that you have a good reason for wanting these objects. If I were to lend them to you, would you tell me your secret?'

'I shall have to consult someone, and when I have done so, I shall return to you,' said Shatir.

He went away, leaving the merchant in a state of high excitement. He knew, after all, that Shatir, by prayers and fasting, and through a long period of self-denial, was trying to attract the attention of the Celestial Powers of Good. Could it be that he needed the objects for their reception?

When Shatir returned, he said, 'Illustrious merchant and good friend! I have consulted with those who know, and I am able to inform you of the reason for my needing the articles about which we have spoken. But here is a condition: you must tell nobody what I am about to impart to you.'

The merchant readily agreed, and Shatir continued:

'You may know that I have for long tried to attract to me, to become their servant, the Celestial Powers of Good. Now, after considerable austerities and sacrifices, I have been told by them that they will descend from the heavens and converse with me. But I must have a suitable place, correctly furnished, for their reception.'

The merchant was delighted, for he hoped that he, too, might benefit from the visit of the Celestial Ones. He lent the carpet and cushions to Shatir. That night he crept out and peered through a crack in the shrine, to see what was happening.

He saw Shatir sitting at one end of the carpet. At the other end were the cushions, and the merchant could plainly see, by the light of a lamp, that the cushions were dented, as if some invisible presence reposed there.

The merchant crept away, and the next day he went to the same place by daylight. He knocked on the door, and Shatir came out.

'How went the interview with the Celestial Ones?' asked the merchant, when Shatir appeared.

'One of them came, and I spoke to him, and he told me many great secrets' answered Shatir. 'His appearance was of such beauty and magnificence that it is invisible to any but the pious and good. He has decided to make my shrine his abode on earth, where he can be seen by those worthy of such an experience. One glimpse of him will transform anyone's destiny so that the observer will be granted felicity and will be numbered among the elect of humankind!'

The merchant begged Shatir to allow him to salute the Celestial

One, and Shatir agreed. The following day the merchant was shown in by the one door, was allowed to bow to the dented cushions, and was ushered out by the other door. His heart was radiant, and although he had seen nothing, he at least knew that he had seen the evidence that the superior being was present, and he almost convinced himself that he had seen him.

By the time he had arrived home, the merchant had embroidered the tales in his own mind. He was also so excited that he forgot his promise, and told his wife. She, in turn, told her maid, who told everyone she knew, and they told others, until the whole town was buzzing with the news.

Presently the town was empty, and all the citizens were on the hilltop, clamouring to be allowed into the shrine.

Shatir appealed to them to be still: and then, one by one, he conducted the people into the Presence, and out again by the other door, as he had done in the case of the merchant.

Now the people of the town, down to the smallest vagrant, believed themselves to be specially singled out for special consideration by the Celestial One, and each agreed that he had in fact seen him, and also that his beauty was indescribable.

Within a fairly short period of time word of this miraculous event reached the ears of the King of the country, who immediately suspected an imposture, for such things often happen. He accordingly sent some of his chamberlains and police, in disguise, to the town, to investigate Shatir and his shrine.

But all their enquiries showed that Shatir led a blameless life, and that he had taken nothing from anyone, except for the loan of the furnishings from the merchant. Everyone in the town stated that they had seen the Celestial Visitor with their own eyes, and that only villains were unable to do so. The investigators went to the shrine. When they returned to the capital city, they informed the King that they, too, had seen what the others had seen, and his Majesty was convinced.

He called Shatir to his court.

Now this was what Shatir had been working for all along, but he made various difficulties and showed himself reluctant; with many a 'What does a poor man want with a King?' until the King was aching to see him.

In his room of private audiences adjoining the throneroom, the King received Shatir and questioned him. 'The reports which your Majesty has received are correct in every detail' said the rogue.

'The one thing which I have which is somewhat tangible, from the Celestial One, is this gorgeous robe which I am wearing, and which astonishes everyone who sets eyes upon it. It is a magical robe as well. Like the Celestial One himself, of course, it is invisible to the impure.'

Now the King could see no robe, but all the same he coveted it as he had never wanted anything in his life. 'A man of your sanctity surely does not need such an object,' he hinted, 'and there would, of course, be compensation if you cared to present it to me. . . .'

'Your Majesty,' said Shatir, 'nothing would please me more. I am only a poor man of the spirit, and you must forgive me for not having thought of that myself. Be pleased to accept the robe, and the compensation will of course be useful, so that I can carry on my charities.'

Affecting to remove the robe from his shoulders, and handling it gently, he moved as if to place it upon the shoulders of the King. He, of course, could not feel anything of the actual robe, which did not exist: but he felt much more, a sense of holy joy.

'Go to the Hall of Assembly' said the King, 'and announce the history and the nature of the robe to the assembled courtiers and representatives of the people. Say that I shall appear in the robe shortly. When I do so, I shall give you your reward publicly.'

Now it happened that there was a Sufi, who had access day or night to the King, and he walked into the private audience chamber in time to hear the transaction. 'Your Majesty', he said, 'may I have a glass of water?'

'Of course' said the King, motioning to a servant to bring one. When it was handed to him, the Sufi threw it over the King, robe and all.

'What are you soaking me for, fool?' shouted the monarch.

'The robe does not impede the effect of water' said the Sufi; 'but there was nothing impure about that water . . . .' Putting his hands to the King's shoulders, he made as if to transfer the robe to his own back. 'Now', he said, 'would your Majesty kindly walk into the assembly hall and see what happens?'

The King entered the hall and the crowd, having been told that he would be wearing the Celestial Robe and therefore imagining that they saw it – or desirous that they should not be thought impure – gasped and cried out, 'Wonderful, look at the colours, look at it, how sublime. . . . .'

The King seated himself on his throne, and the Sufi entered the hall shortly afterwards. But, although the Sufi was 'wearing the robe', and everyone saw him come in, nobody applauded, nobody cheered, nothing whatever was said.

The Sufi stood up and said: 'May I be the sacrifice of your Majesty! The people have seen the wondrous Robe, and the King's Majesty wearing it. It has been brought by the Venerable Shatir, who stands here and who is to be rewarded with a sum for his

182

charities.

'I shall now request His Majesty to present a hundred thousand gold pieces to the Venerable Shatir.'

He placed a cloth bag in the King's hands.

'Celestial robes are so rare that they should be paid for with celestial gold, of course.'

And the King handed the empty bag to Shatir, who took it with as good a grace as he could.

But there are still people, all over the kingdom, who think that the Celestial One really did come as a result of the devoutness of Shatir. Since all this happened many years ago, even more people now revere the name of the Great Shatir, and his shrine is still a place of pilgrimage.

The Magic Pocket

Once upon a time there were three brothers who lived in a village in a far-away land. Because this community was so isolated and few strangers were seen there, its people used to call themselves, simply, 'The People'.

Of the brothers, Adil was the eldest, Amin the second, and Arif the youngest.

One fine day the three were sitting by the wayside, when they saw a traveller approaching. When he came up to them, after salutations, he began to reveal strange news.

'There is a King of a certain country, far from here,' he told the three, 'whose beautiful daughter, the Princess Nafisa, has an insatiable craving for figs. She eats them by day and she eats them by night. Walking and talking, sitting or lying, she stuffs herself with figs. Figs, figs, figs, fresh or dried.

'Nobody will marry her because of this. The King, whose name is Abd-al-Aali, has decreed that whoever can cure her, providing that he is a fitting consort, may become her husband, and shall inherit the whole Kingdom in due course.'

Now the hearts of the three brothers were aroused by this strange tale, and they asked the stranger the name of the country of King Abd-al-Aali.

'It is called Acacia-country' he said, 'but the route to it is difficult. If you are proposing to seek the lady's hand, I suggest you at least prepare yourselves with a suitable stratagem.'

He went on his way, and the brothers excitedly discussed their prospects of finding, curing and marrying the Princess Nafisa. After a great deal of argument, they came to the conclusion that the best way to treat this ailment was to feed the patient so many figs that she would become revolted at the mere sight of them, for ever afterwards.

Luckily there was no shortage of the fruit: for the brothers lived in a fig-growing area. 'It is my right to attempt this exploit' said the eldest brother. So the others helped him to collect a truly enormous basket-load of succulent figs, which he strapped to his back. It reached from the top of his head almost to his heels: but, as he was very strong, Adil was able to carry the load at a fair pace.

He set off along the road in the direction from which the traveller had come, and after many miles he came across a poor dervish dozing in a dry ditch. The holy man stirred at his approach, and, seeing Adil, called out:

'Son of good fortune! Where are you going, and what have you got in that great basket?'

'I am seeking the Land of the Acacia' said Adil, 'and in this basket are figs, which I plan to feed to the Princess Nafisa, so that she will become surfeited with them and thus be cured of her fig-addiction, making me eligible for her hand in marriage and subsequently to have the inheritance of the domain of King Abd-al-Aali, her father.'

The dervish said: 'It is well that people with enterprise and courage should follow the road to success and fulfilment with optimism, and regardless of possible terrors. Thus have the ignorant often become wise, and thus have the humble frequently been rewarded, and thus, too, have the people of old been able to preserve, for those of us who come after, the knowledge of the rewards of effort and dedication.'

'Thank you,' said Adil politely, 'but can you not help me? What, for instance, is the way to Acacia-Land?'

The dervish said: 'Acacia-Land can be found by following this path: always turning when it turns, and never turning when it does not turn, and refusing to be beguiled by those things which are not of the road. And I can tell you more, for you have a difficult enterprise ahead of you. But before I do that, you will have to give me some of your figs, for I am hungry and the due needs of the body must always be accommodated.'

Adil thought for a moment, weighing up the alternatives, and seeking the just answer: for his name means 'Justice'. Finally he said:

'Honoured Sir! I have applied my logical capacities to your

184

remarks, and find that I cannot give you any figs. This is because I have only a limited quantity of them, and I have far to go. It is perfectly possible that, when I give these figs to the Princess, I might fail in my mission through being even one fig short. Therefore I must leave you to your own resources, and must dispense with your further advice. In any case, a man should be able to proceed on the minimum of help from others.'

So saying, he went on his way.

When, after overcoming many hazards and undergoing numerous adventures and trials, Adil arrived at the Palace of the the monarch of Acacia-Land, he was immediately shown into the presence of Princess Nafisa. She was delighted to see his enormous basket of figs, and set to without delay, gobbling them up as fast as she could. They were delicious. In almost less time than it takes to tell, however, she had finished the lot and was loudly demanding more.

Poor Adil was sorrowingly shown the door.

When, again after many a tribulation, Adil arrived home, the second brother, Amin, whose name means 'True', resolved to try his luck.

Amin set off with a similar basket of figs, but he also took beside him a donkey laden with as many figs as it could carry. Altogether he had three or four times the quantity of fruit that Adil had taken to the Princess.

It was not long before he saw the very same dervish, walking slowly, supported by his staff, along the road.

'Good day to you, O One of Bright Prospects!' said the dervish. He added: 'You are well laden with figs. Would you fill this begging-bowl with a handful of them?'

Amin thought for a moment, and then he replied: 'Venerable Man of The Way! I have considered your request. My name is Amin, and I am a man of truth. In truth, if I were to start giving away figs at this early stage, I would have none left to sate the Princess Nafisa. I am determined to accomplish what my brother Adil has failed to do: to make the Princess loathe figs, so that she will marry me, so that I may become successor to King Abd-al-Aali, of Acacia-Land.'

And he went on his way, convinced that principles were principles, in his interpretation of them, at any rate.

When, at length, and with just as many pleasant and unhappy experiences as those of his brother, Amin arrived at the Royal Palace of Acacia-Land, he found that the Princess's appetite, fed on more and more figs as people brought them from far and wide, had become even greater. It took her only a few minutes to dispose of his entire stock. After that he had to take to his heels, because she complained bitterly that he was being stingy in only offering her that miserable quantity, and vowed that she would command that he be shut up in a dungeon, if he did not bring her more.

And so Amin the True, like his brother Adil the Just before him, made his way sadly home. This, of course, left only Arif, the Wise (which is what *his* name means) who was as determined as they to win the Princess Nafisa's hand.

Arif collected figs and dried them. Then he found the largest and hardiest donkey in the village and loaded it up. In this way he nearly doubled the load which Amin the True had carried. He also said to himself: 'Having done all this, I must also keep aware of any possibility which might help my undertaking on the way.'

Not long after he had started along the highway, Arif the Wise, in his turn also came upon the dervish, and told him his plan. The dervish said: 'O Laden-down Man of Enterprise! Give me your hand, and give me a couple of figs, for the way is hard for ancient travellers.'

'Willingly' said Arif, 'You can have all my figs, for all I care, if you can only tell me how I can win the Princess Nafisa...'

'That's a bargain!' shouted the dervish. 'Now, you should know that my name is the Dervish Ajib-o-Gharib, which means Strange and Extraordinary. You give me all the figs and the donkey, and I will give you something very much more useful, however 'strange and extraordinary' it may seem to you at this moment.'

Arif agreed. The dervish took a piece of cloth, and sewed it upon the outside of Arif's robe. 'This is now a pocket' he said, 'and you will place in it only this single dried fig. When you arrive in the Princess's presence, hand it to her. The pocket will, while she is chewing it, immediately replenish itself with another dried fig, and so on. The supply of figs will be endless.'

Arif thanked the ancient and continued on his way. After a number of adventures every bit as strange and miscellaneous as those of his brothers, he reached the Palace of Acacia-Land. He had some difficulty getting to see the Princess Nafisa, it is true, since few of the numerous guards, courtiers and assorted loungers there believed that there was any point in presenting her with a single fig, which was all that the youth seemed to have with him.

But everything went as the dervish Ajib-o-Gharib had foretold. The Princess grabbed Arif's fig and started to chew it, holding out her hand for another. As soon as she did so, another fig appeared in the pocket, and Arif gave it to her. And this went on, and on, all day, all night, and most of the next day as well. In the end, the Princess made a gesture of disgust. 'Ugh!' she said 'I have had enough figs. Stop giving them to me. I never want to see another fig as long as I live.'

Sure enough, she was cured, as everyone found out when day after day passed without the Princess asking for a single fig.

Now the King, whose name Abd-al-Aali means Servant of the Highest, said to Arif:

'Young man, you have passed the test of the figs, and we are grateful to you. The Princess, I am told, is prepared to marry you. But there is still the matter of the second part of the requirement. You may recall that we have announced that the suitor must not only stop the Princess eating figs, but must also be a fitting consort to inherit the Kingdom. This means that I have to add various tests.'

Arif answered that he was indeed prepared to continue. By now he was in love with the Princess and wanted to inherit the Kingdom as well.

'Mighty King, Essence of Royalty: Command and I shall obey; for is it not said that in the presence of kings the essential words are: "Hearing is the same as obedience?" '

'Obedience is possible only to the extent of one's capacity' said the King, gravely, 'and that is what we have to test. First you must find two witnesses.'

Before the wedding could take place, there would have to be found, by the custom of that country, two witnesses who were not related to the bride or groom. But the country of Acacia-Land was by now inhabited by only two kinds of people: those who wanted to marry the Princess and therefore refused to help anyone else do so, and those who had been convinced that the Princess could never be cured and would not believe it, now, even if they had proof.

So nobody would be a witness.

Arif walked back down the highway until he came to where he had seen the dervish Ajib-o-Gharib. There he was, sitting by the roadside.

The dervish, without preliminaries, said: 'Don't start telling me that you need this and you need that. If you know that I can help you, you must do as I say. Now, are you ready?'

'I am ready' answered Arif.

The dervish said: 'Here is a sign. Make it when you are talking to people, and they will believe you, if what you say is true and if they are themselves just.'

Arif thanked him and returned to the capital of Acacia-Land. He soon found two witnesses, and they went with him to the King.

'Now,' said his Majesty, 'you have to obtain the ring. It takes three people to get it, and it has to be brought to you by a bird in the forest.'

The three set off for a nearby forest, with nothing to help them

187

but their friendship and the signal which the dervish had taught Arif. After they had looked everywhere for the ring or the bird, Arif thought of the pocket. He put his hand into it, and found a small flute there. Taking it out, he blew a note on it, and suddenly a bird fluttered down, with a ring in its beak. It alighted on the hand of one of the witnesses, and presented the ring to the other one. Then it flew away.

Now the three went back to the King and showed him the ring.

'You have passed that test,' he said, 'and now all you have to do is to pass the test of "occasion and perception." Here are four lambs. Take them into the fields and graze them for four weeks. After that, bring them back to me, for they are the symbol of our prosperity.'

Arif took the lambs into the fields. The first night his two witnesses came under cover of darkness and stole one of them. The second night, the King came in disguise and offered Arif a hundred thousand gold pieces for one of the lambs, but he refused. The following day, the dervish appeared.

'One of my lambs is lost' said Arif, and told him the whole story.

The dervish gave him a design inscribed on parchment and said: 'Wave this in the air, and your lamb will always be returned to you.'

Arif tried it, and, sure enough, the lamb which the witnesses had taken suddenly appeared. After that the King came back again, disguised as a bandit, and threatened Arif with death if he did not give him the lambs. Arif handed them over. Soon afterwards, however, he waved his design and they returned to him. Then, one after another, the Princess and one member of the royal Court after another, appeared in disguise, cajoling, threatening and pleading, all asking for lambs. Arif obliged them all, and made sure that he always got them back with his magical diagram.

When his time was up, Arif returned to the Palace, and the King said:

'You have passed all the tests except that of perception. Who were the people who threatened, cajoled and tempted you when you were in the fields?'

'Why, Sir,' said Arif, 'They were you yourself, the two witnesses, the Princess and various members of the Royal Court.'

And that was how Arif became husband to the Princess Nafisa, which means 'Little Soul', and eventually King of Acacia-Land, which translates as *Balad as-Salam*: 'Land of Peace or Completion'.

In the original language of this story, the word for 'Pocket' *(jaib)* also means 'Heart'; and the word for 'Fig' sounds very similar to the word for 'Clay,' *(tin)* the earth and hence for things which surround us.......

The Son of a Story-Teller

Once upon a time there was a story-teller, who was of a long line of bards, whose tradition was that they preserved and related the tales of olden times at the court of a certain king.

Now this reciter was proud of his ancient lineage, and of the extent of his repertoire, and of the degree of wisdom of his tales, for they were used as indicators of the present, as records of the past, and as allusions to the things of the world of sense and of the world beyond appearances alike.

But at the court, too, as is natural and useful, were other experts of all kinds. There were military chiefs, courtiers, advisers and ambassadors; there were engineers skilled in building and in demolishing, men of religion and of other kinds of learning: in short, there were people of every type and condition, and each one of them thought himself better than all the others.

One day, when there had been a long dispute about precedence among these worthy people, the only conclusion at which they could arrive was that, of all of them, the story-teller was the least important, the least useful, the least skilled in any measurable art. The assembly therefore decided that, to begin the process of reducing the number of worthless people around them, they would eliminate the story-teller. Each one also thought, privately, to himself, 'When we have got rid of *him,* we will be able, one by one, to prove that all the others are superfluous: and then *I* will be left – and *I* shall be the king's sole adviser!'

It was against this background that a select delegation of the courtiers went to the story-teller and said:

'We have been deputed by the rest of the lords of the realm who attend upon His Majesty to inform you that we have decided that of all those associated with the court, you are the most superfluous. You do not go to war, to ensure the glory of the kingdom or to extend our victorious monarch's dominions. You do not judge cases, to preserve the tranquillity of the state. You do not minister to the serenity of the people's souls, as do the religious chiefs. You are not handsome, like the elegant boon-companions. In short,

189

you are nothing at all!'

'Venerable and respected peacocks of wisdom and pillars of faith!' cried the story-teller, 'far be it from me to disagree with anything which you might have resolved; but, since it is incumbent upon me to tell the truth in court affairs, out of loyalty to His Majesty, I have the following representation to make:

'There is an ancient and deeply wise tale which completely proves that, far from being unnecessary, the reciter of tales is absolutely essential to the well-being and the power of the empire. If you allow me to narrate it, I shall be glad to do so.'

The delegation of courtiers were not anxious to let the man have his say; but, at that moment the King called everyone back into the throne-room and demanded to know what had been going on. When he heard what we have just heard, he commanded the story-teller to begin his tale, omitting no detail.

The story-teller began:

'Peacock of the Earth! Fountain of Wisdom! Great Majesty and Shadow of Allah upon Earth! Know that once, in the most remote times there was a king, like your own Majesty a just and powerful sovereign, esteemed in many lands, beloved of his people and feared by his enemies.

'This king had three beautiful daughters, fair as the moon. One day the three went for a walk in the woods near the palace, and they completely disappeared.

'Extensive searches were made for them, but no trace of them was to be found. After many days the king ordered the heralds to cry: "In the King's name! Let none say that he did not hear! Anyone who can find the three daughters of His Majesty and can restore them safe and sound to our benign and sagacious monarch's household will be rewarded with the hand in marriage of whichever one he may desire!"

'Still, for weeks and months nothing was heard: it was as if the earth had opened and swallowed the girls up.

'Then, when all hope seemed at an end, the king called his courtiers together, including the lords spiritual, military and temporal, and the judges of all the judges, and all the quality and chivalry of the state. He addressed them thus:

'"Reverend doctors of the law and of faith! Lions and tigers of the all-conquering armies! Relentless punishers of miscreants and kings of the arts of trade and industry!

'"Hear and know my command. You shall elect from among yourselves representatives, two or three in number, who shall set off in search of the lost princesses, and shall not return without them. Those who have been chosen shall inherit the kingdom if they are successful. If they fail, they shall not set foot in our dominions again, on pain of death."

'The assembled court immediately divided into groups to elect representatives, and they in turn nominated and voted for their own deputies, until it emerged that two men had been chosen. These were the blood-drinking commander of the ever-victorious armies, the Emir Al-Jaish, and the wisest man in all the land, the Prime Minister, known as the Wazir Al-Wuzura.

'The king gave them a final lecture, after which they touched their heads, hearts and eyes, murmuring: "To hear is to obey!" They then sprang to the saddle and rode headlong out of the palace gate, as trumpets blared to announce their departure.

'Now they journeyed and travelled, walked and rode, encountered many hardships and, in a word, did everything which their combined valour and sagacity could devise. But, before they found any trace of the missing princesses, they were captured by bandits and sold as slaves to the owner of an inn, who worked them like beasts of burden, making them look after the men and animals of the travellers who passed that way.

'When no news of the mission had been received for a very long time, and the King and his court were plunged into the deepest gloom, a certain young story-teller, son of a story-teller, himself the son of a story-teller, and the son of one who was also a story-teller, for uncounted generations, came to the court. He appealed to the King to allow him to go in search of the maidens.

'At first the king refused to allow him to go, wondering what a mere teller of tales could do where two of the very best men in the kingdom had evidently failed. But in the end, realising that he could not in any case make things worse, he gave him leave.

'The story-teller leapt upon a horse and sped, fast as an arrow, in the direction of the rising sun. After many adventures he came upon an inn and there he saw, miserably waiting on the guests, dressed in rags and with their feet in shackles, the shuffling figures of none other than the Emir and the Wazir. When they recognised him, the pair pleaded piteously for help; and he was able to pay their ransom-money to the innkeeper and secured their freedom, buying them decent clothes.

'They were, at first, disconcerted to hear that this, to them, relatively humble man, bore the King's commission to join in the search; and they were chagrined to know that such as he could release them from captivity, for their arrogance was fast returning. In the end, however, they had to agree to his continuing with them on the quest.

'They continued on their way, not knowing where they were bound, until, at nightfall, they came to a small hovel where a poor old woman was sitting, mending a reed-basket by the door. The

191

story-teller stopped; and they all sat down to talk. After sharing the woman's poor supper, the story-teller told a tale of long ago to entertain the others, and the woman asked them what their business was in those parts.

'"We are three members of the court of our king, and we are on a quest for the three beautiful daughters of His Majesty, who disappeared many months ago" they told her. "But, so far, we have neither seen them nor heard a word about them, although we have been through many difficulties."

'"Ah", said the woman, "I may be able to help you in that, since you show me that you are wise by the tale which you have recited, and I think that you may have a chance, but just a small chance, of success.

'"The three princesses have been captured by three evil genii and carried to the bottom of a lake near here. They have a magical underwater palace there, and it is next to impossible for humankind to penetrate it."

'After spending a fitful night's sleep beside the hovel, the three set off for the lake. It was surrounded by trees covered in twisted vines, and a feeling of evil loomed over the place.

'"I shall go down first" said the chief of the warriors, "for I am the strongest and can deal with any kind of foe. What can a minister and a poet do in a case like this!" He twirled his moustaches in a gesture of vainglory, and removed most of his clothes. The others made ropes out of the vines and the soldier, sword bared and clutched in his right hand, started to descend into the water. "If I tug" he said, "haul me up."

'As he went down into the water, he found that it got colder and colder, and suddenly there was a sound like a thousand crashing rolls of thunder coming from the dark depths. Fear gripped his heart, and the once-gallant warrior tugged agitatedly to be pulled up again.

'Then the minister insisted on going down, for he coveted, like so many administrators, the power that would come to him if he could only wed one of the king's own daughters.

'But the same thing happened, and he had to be pulled back to dry land again.

'Then the story-teller went down. The water was cold, but he steeled himself against it. The noise was as loud as a thousand thunderstorms, but he managed to close his ears to it. Finally, when he thought that he would have to give up, he found that he had dropped beyond the protective spells of the genies and was in a huge underwater cavern.

'He opened a door and came to a room where the first thing he saw was one of the princesses, sitting on the floor, with a hideous-looking genie in the shape of a serpent with eighteen heads, sprawling asleep in one corner.

'The story-teller snatched a gleaming sword which hung on the wall, and with one blow cut off the heads of the evil one. The princess kissed his hand, and round his neck she placed a royal chain of office. "Where are your sisters?" asked the young man. She opened another door, and within the room beyond lay the second princess, guarded by a sleeping genie in the shape of a gigantic skull, with tiny legs.

'The story-teller pulled a jewelled dagger from a bracket in the wall, and with one blow severed the hideous head from the legs, and the genie expired with a groan. Then the three went into the next room, where they found the youngest sister, guarded by a genie with a vulture's head and a lizard's body. Instantly he saw that the evil thing was asleep, the youth picked up a garrotte which was hung on the wall, and strangled the genie to death. The two princesses placed a crown on his head and a sword of state in his hand.

'Now they hurried back to the place where the rope of vines hung down into the cavern, and the story-teller made the first princess hold onto it, while he tugged with the signal to be drawn up. The first princess reached the shore in safety.

'Then the second princess was lifted up, and the rope came down for the last girl. "Go up" said the story-teller, but the princess said, "You should go, for I fear treachery. You could be left down here if we three are all safely taken up, for your companions could then claim the reward and leave you behind."

'But the young man refused to go first, and so did the princess. After a time, the two men above decided to take the two princesses and to return to the court to claim the prize that rightfully belonged to their deserted comrade.

'The villains threatened the two girls that if they did not support their story that they were the real heroes, they would be killed.

'Thus it was that the four arrived back at the palace and were received like conquerors. They told the king that the youngest princess had been killed in the cave, and he ordered that forty days' mourning was to be observed, after which the Emir and the Minister were to be married to the two girls whom they were supposed to have rescued.

'Meanwhile, deep in the genies' cavern, the young man and the youngest princess realised that they had been abandoned when the rope did not come down for the last time.

'They looked through all the rooms, and in one of them came across a jewel-studded brass box. When the princess opened the lid, a voice said:

'"What is your command? I am the spirit of this box. Ask and it shall be granted!"

'The story-teller at once asked to be transported, with the box, to the surface of the lake and then to the shore: which was done in the twinkling of an eye. Then he asked for a huge ship loaded with treasures, and the sword, crown and chain of office to be emblazoned upon the sails. When he and the princess were aboard, he ordered it to fly instantly to the harbour just beside the palace of the princess's father.

'When he saw the ship, the King thought:

'"This is the vessel of a mighty monarch, and I shall myself approach him to do him honour, for he has three symbols of royalty on his sails, and he must therefore be three times as important as I."

'The King then went on board the ship and began to speak to the story-teller with great humility, not recognising him in the robes and jewels which he had obtained through the magical box.

'But the princess, unable to restrain her joy, jumped out of concealment and told her father the whole story. Then the evil minister and soldier were banished from the realm, and the story-teller married the princess, to inherit, with her, the kingdom in the fullness of time.

'This, noble sirs, shows you', continued the story-teller, 'how important a story-teller can be.'

Finding the Teaching

Q: *I first came across your books in 1975. This was when I read Paul Theroux's best-seller* The Great Railway Bazaar. *May I quote from it? Theroux has just met a curiously-dressed 'Seeker after Truth' on a train in Turkey, heading for the Far East. He had the 'aspiring prophet' look, and 'His shirt had been artistically cut from a flour sack and he wore a very faded pair of 'Washington Brand' bib overalls, an elephant-hair bracelet on one wrist, and an Indian bangle on the other. I had seen him sitting in a lotus position in second class. He put a worn book by Idries Shah on the table; it had the chewed-over look Korans have in the the hands of the languid fanatics I saw later in the holy city of Meshed. But he did not read it.'*

As soon as I read this I remembered that similar books, that I had taken little notice of, were in the hands and on the shelves of dozens of 'spiritually-minded' people wandering all over the world, and especially in the possession of people who imagine that they can be enlightened from them or teach from them. Since then I have found that there is an industry, so to speak, of people who use your books like this. What is to be done about them?

A: First of all you must remember that there are also other readers of the books. These are people in all kinds of disciplines, and also people who are indeed sincere seekers who are not show-offs like the one you mention. As for the show-offs and the self-appointed 'teachers', quite a number of them come to understand, in due course, that the books have a special use and that when they have read them they have to continue along the specially organised path for which they are a preparation. At any given time there will be plenty of people at the early stages, both as 'learners' and 'teachers' who are using these books in this silly and superficial way. At the same time, there are also plenty of people who are freeing themselves from this inadequate posture. You may not see them, but we do, as they come to us.

Q: *Yes, I see that, but how are they to come to this understanding, and how can they get in touch with you?*

A: If they really want to learn, they come to the understanding all right. If they need the orientation which is not available through books, they only have to write to us. Every copy of every book has the publisher's address in it, at the front: and people write care of such addresses.

A PERFUMED SCORPION

The 'Perfuming of a Scorpion' is the image employed by the sage, Bahaudin Naqshband, to symbolise hypocrisy and self-deception: both in the individual and in institutions.

The lectures and meditations in this book examine the Perfume and the Scorpion: the overlay and the underlying reality – in psychology, human behaviour and the learning process itself.

". . . . . combining straight instruction, information, humour, aphorisms, verses. . . . An invigorating, abrasive book like jumping into icy water – hard to do, but you're glad you've done it."

Books and Bookmen

Other books by Idries Shah.

TALES OF THE DERVISHES

'These are teaching stories, spanning more than 1,000 years, from Persian, Arabic and Turkish traditional collections – published and in manuscript – and from oral sources, which include contemporary teaching centres; chosen and arranged by a Sufi to present to Westerners a Sufi view of life: one that challenges our intellectual assumptions at almost every point.'
The Observer

'An astonishingly generous and liberating book ... strikingly appropriate for our time and situation.'
The Sunday Times

'Stories which equal, and sometimes surpass, in relevance, piquancy and humour, the best of the spiritual and ethical teachers of the West ... source-book of authentic teaching-stories.'
Kirkus Review

'Beautifully translated . . . equips men and women to make good use of their lives.'
Professor James Kritzeck: *The Nation*

NEGLECTED ASPECTS
OF SUFI STUDY

Based on University lectures 'Neglected Aspects of Sufi Study' deals with many of the problems of Sufi methods of study, those that is which militate against its effective progress in the modern world . . . notably the unrecognised assumptions which we make about ourselves and about learning and its processes.

This book provides a companion to the twenty volumes of Sufi studies and literature which Shah has extracted from the literature and practice of Sufis over the past one thousand years.

'It elaborates points found particularly difficult in our culture because of sets of mind.'

Books and Bookmen

A VEILED GAZELLE:
SEEING HOW TO SEE

As the great mystic Ibn Arabi explains in his 'Interpreter of Desires', 'A Veiled Gazelle' is a subtlety, an organ of higher perception.

Sufi experientialists refer to the activation of these centres of awareness as the awakening of real knowledge of Truth beyond form.

This book deals with the symbolical and instrumental employment in Sufi studies of its literature: which is seldom didactic and never meant only as entertainment, although regarded in all cultures as some of the world's greatest writing.

199

Other books by Idries Shah.

CARAVAN OF DREAMS

'One can read a story or two and be delighted. But the effect does not stop there. These stories adhere, return, seeming somehow to expand after reading into an area beyond outer consciousness. Like fine poems . . . like great poems . . . more than rewarding, and impossible to forget.'

Tribune

'Like a fabled caravan from another time, this book travels great distances . . . re-stimulates the dream, by indicating real possibilities and practical alternatives to our present ways of operation; presenting not idle fantasies but signals from the tradition of known and tested activity; relevant, fruitful and urgent for our present society.'

New Society

Other books by Idries Shah.

THE HUNDRED TALES OF WISDOM

Tales, anecdotes and narratives used in Sufi schools for the development of insights beyond ordinary perceptions, presented by Idries Shah, and translated from the Persian. Traditionally known as 'The Hundred Tales of Wisdom' the stories are of the life, teachings and miracles of Jalaludin Rumi from Aflaki's 'Munaqib', together with certain important tales from Rumi's works.

SPECIAL ILLUMINATION: THE SUFI USE OF HUMOUR

Idries Shah is well known for his publishing of the Nasrudin corpus of teaching stories, in which humour is used to display human behaviour and also to engage the mind in a different manner. 'Special Illumination' is the phrase used by the great teacher and mystic Jalaludin Rumi to stress the importance of humour in metaphysical experience.

'Many jokes in "Special Illumination" are collected from or set in the west . . . he demonstrates that we have perhaps failed to appreciate, or even notice, our own instructional riches.'

New Society

THE WAY OF THE SUFI

'The definitive account of ancient Sufi teaching. A great many common Western distortions and misinterpretations are cleared away, and much valuable source material anthologized.'

Tribune

'A present for anyone who, though religious, finds the current orthodoxies unpalatable.'

Times Literary Supplement

'Highly educative, basic course of study; intrinsic relevance to all.'

The Hindu

'A key book ... can assist to demonstrate other possible uses of the mind ... gives new material on method, history, personnel, much of it from oral sources.'

The Observer

Other books by Idries Shah.

SPECIAL PROBLEMS IN THE STUDY OF SUFI IDEAS

This important monograph constitutes the whole text of Idries Shah's Seminar at Sussex University, fully annotated, indexed and with a bibliography and notes.

It knits together the available knowledge about Sufi thought and literature in its passage through many deforming influences, such as the development of cults, the misinterpretation by literalist scholars, and the fallacious comparisons of committed 'specialists'.

'Masterful essay ... he has ably presented Sufism to the West and has conveyed its deep sense of reality to modern man ...'

Professor A. Reza Arasteh,
Psychology of the Sufi Way, 1972.

Other books by Idries Shah.

REFLECTIONS

This selection of Idries Shah's own fables, aphorisms and teachings is now in its third edition and continues to be extremely popular.

Pocket-sized, it is immensely entertaining and at the same time offers an alternative view of our society that is both refreshing and profitable.

'More wisdom than I have found in any other book this year.'

Pat Williams *Review of the Year, BBC*.

'It seems to oblige the mind to scorn the satisfaction of going from A to B in favour of an approach from a different angle, taking in unsuspected territory, hatches out as modified behaviour.'

Evening News

THE EXPLOITS OF THE INCOMPARABLE MULLA NASRUDIN

The first collection of Nasrudin stories acclaimed as a humourous masterpiece, as a collection of the finest jokes, as a priceless gift book, and for its hundred 'enchanted tales'.

But this folklore figure's antics have also been divined as 'mirroring the antics of the mind'. They have a double use: significance starts to sink in. Idries Shah has achieved a true breakthrough with a book which can convulse on the level of humour and still get serious reviews, like this one from the sociological journal *New Society*:

'His stories are perfectly designed, harmless models for isolating and holding for a moment the distortions of the mind which so often pass for reasonable behaviour.'

'Arouse laughter in the simple and contemplation in the illuminated'
– The Listener

'Sharp English that doesn't waste a word'
– Sunday Telegraph

'Our familiar responses are ruled out'
– New Statesman

'All will welcome the telling by Idries Shah'
– Times Educational Supplement

Other books by Idries Shah.

LEARNING HOW TO LEARN

'"Learning How to Learn" is both the distillation of a million words and a guide to the whole body of the Shah materials. Certain irresistible keys keep the reader on the edge of the seat.'
'A book which surely marks the watershed in studies of the mind.'

Psychology Today Choice of the Month

'Bracing and often shocking. Shah's approach can best be described as a brisk and informed commonsense at its highest level.'

Books and Bookmen

'Packed with important information.'

New Society

Other books by Idries Shah.

THE ELEPHANT IN THE DARK

Rumi's elephant was examined in the dark by men using only one sense – that of touch. In contact with only one part of it, they described it variously as pillars (the legs), rope (the tail), a fan (the ear), agreeing only on its texture.

Christian scholars examining Sufism often say that Sufi theories are close to Christianity. Many Moslems maintain that they are derived from Islam. Other religions too find evidence of derivation in Sufi ideas. The Islamic interpretation is that religion is of one origin.

The materials in this book deal with the interplay between Christianity, Islam and the Sufi conception of surrender to God.

Other books by Idries Shah.

THE BOOK OF THE BOOK

'This is a handsome, red-and-gold volume which is easy on the eye and weighs satisfactorily in the hand. It is a brief, dense, ancient tale of a book, of the book of that book, what it gave, and what people were able to take from it. The unalerted reader, turning page after page, may wonder if it is a joke.

Actually it is – among other things – an extraordinary psychological test, in that it predicts the complete range of possible responses to itself.'

Sunday Telegraph

'Beyond words' (*The Observer*); 'Something new for the West' (*The Guardian*); 'Tantalizing' (*World Medicine*); 'Shattered the literary world' (*Irish Press*); 'Astonishing' (*Sunday Mirror*); 'Looks legit' (*The Arizona Republic*).

Other books by Idries Shah.

WISDOM OF THE IDIOTS

Narratives of the action-philosophy of the thinkers who called themselves 'idiots' in contrast to the self-styled 'wise'. The first edition of this book was widely acclaimed for its entertainment value and psychological interest.

The celebrated writer Nina Epton said in a recent broadcast:

'Seeds that Idries Shah sows on our Western path are chosen by a discerning modern mind, with a profound knowledge of the East and West. The best spiritual traditions, interpreted afresh, are applied by Idries Shah to our contemporary world. This is his contribution to our spiritual equipment – which consequently now finds itself considerably enriched.'

'Opens up a new world of understanding'
– The Inquirer

'Rare examples of non-linear thinking'
– Evening News

Other books by Idries Shah.

THE NATIVES ARE RESTLESS

How the English see themselves – their view contrasted with that of people from other countries trying to understand their strange behaviour. Shah also speculates on the likely continuing effect of Englishness on the future development of global society, offering unsuspected parallels between English attitudes and oriental wisdom.

'... I can't imagine anyone not enjoying this many-angled book, such a rich mix of anecdote, information ... and history ...'

– Daily Telegraph

Other books by Idries Shah.

THE DERMIS PROBE

The title-story, with script by Idries Shah, filmed as a space-satire, was chosen as an Outstanding Film of the Year and selected for showing at both the London and New York film festivals. This is a collection of extracts from the written and oral tradition of Eastern thinkers.

Shah says in his Preface:

'In this book you can find illustrated some of the peculiarities of thought in the Country which is today's world, seen by its inhabitants and by those who call themselves visitors.'

'... a peep-show into a world which most people do not know exists'.

— *The Guardian*

'... deftly done, in the true Sufi tradition'.

— *The Times Literary Supplement*

'... whisking away the rug from under our favourite convictions and thinking habits ... the effect is exhilarating'.

— *Tribune*

Other books by Idries Shah.

THE SUFIS

'Many forlorn puzzles in the world, which seemed to suggest that some great spiritual age somewhere in the Middle East had long since died and left indecipherable relics, suddenly come to organic life in this book.'

Ted Hughes: *The Listener*

'Sufism is . . . "the inner secret teaching that is concealed within every religion". The book has flashes of what (without intending to define the word) I can only call illumination.'

D. J. Enright: *New Statesman*

'Fully authoritative' (*Afghanistan News*); 'Important historically and culturally' (*Los Angeles Times*); 'Incredibly rich in scope and fine detail' (*Psychology Today*); 'The definitive statement of Sufism' (*Library Journal*); 'Now its influence is spreading where long overdue' (*The American Scholar*); 'More extraordinary the more it is studied' (*Encounter*); 'Most comprehensively informative' (*New York Times Book Review*).

Other books by Idries Shah.

THE PLEASANTRIES OF THE INCREDIBLE MULLA NASRUDIN

Both this book – containing no less than 165 tales – and the previous Nasrudin volume have been acclaimed for their humour by critics all over the world. Nasrudin tales have been used to illustrate abstruse concepts in high-energy physics: and a complete system of mystical training based upon them was described in the *Hibbert Journal*.

'Parallel to the mind's workings'

– The Observer

'A rare gift – healing laughter' *– New Society*

'Undebased wisdom – an extension of the proverbial'
– Country Life

Other books by Idries Shah.

DARKEST ENGLAND

'... Idries Shah explains the English to themselves and
to others with humour and insight. Using the etymol-
ogy of the English language itself, scholarly research
and a rich store of anecdotes – which serve as teaching
notes – Shah investigates the origins and character of
this strangely oriental tribe and comes to some surpris-
ing and provocative conclusions. A fascinating and enjoyable read ...'

– BBC

'... Full of insights and information assembled to
present a view no English person could easily reach.
Very funny ...'

– Sunday Times

'... trying to tell us something useful ... a darker
edge. Shah knows, and we know, that the foreigner's
problem has become ours; how to be English ...'

– New Society